WALSH

a play by Sharon Pollock

Published with assistance from the Canada Council.

Talonbooks
P.O. Box 2076, Vancouver, British Columbia, Canada V6B 3S3
www.talonbooks.com

Printed and bound in Canada by Hignell Book Printing.

12th Revised Printing: January 2006

Canadian Cataloguing in Publication Data

Pollock, Sharon
    Walsh

    Originally published: Vancouver: Talonbooks, 1973
    ISBN 0-88922-215-0

    1. Sitting Bull, Dakota Chief, 1831–1890 –
Drama. 2. Walsh, James Morrow, 1840–1905 –
Drama. I. Title.
PS8581.O44W3 1983   C812'.54   C83-091363-7
PR9199.3.P64W3 1983

ISBN-10 0-88922-215-0
ISBN-13 978-0-88922-215-1

Walsh was first performed at Theatre Calgary in Calgary, Alberta on November 7, 1973, with the following cast:

Harry	Frank J. Adamson
Clarence	Hardee T. Lineham
Louis	Jean Archambault
Walsh	Michael Fletcher
Mrs. Anderson	Margaret Barton
Crow Eagle	Stephen Russell
McCutcheon	Ron Chudley
Gall	Denis Lacroix
Sitting Bull	August Schellenberg
White Dog	Nolan Jennings
Crowfoot	Frank Turningrobe, Jr.
Colonel MacLeod	Hutchinson Shandro

Directed by Harold G. Baldridge
Set and Lighting Design by Richard Roberts
Costume Design by Jane Grose

Walsh was also performed at the Third Stage of the Stratford Festival in Stratford, Ontario on July 24, 1974, with the following cast:

Harry	J. Kenneth Campbell
Clarence	John Stewart
Louis	Jonathan Welsh
Walsh	Michael Ball
Mrs. Anderson	Donna Farron
Crow Eagle	Terry Judd
McCutcheon	David Hemblen
Gall	John Bayliss
Sitting Bull	Derek Ralston
White Dog	Terry Judd
Crowfoot	Tim Jones
Colonel MacLeod	John Bayliss
Pretty Plume	Donna Farron
Mary	Donna Farron

Directed by John Wood
Designed by John Ferguson
Music and Sound by Alan Laing
Technical Engineering Charles Richmond

LIST OF CHARACTERS

HARRY, *a wagon master.*
CLARENCE, *a new recruit to the NWMP.*
LOUIS, *a Metis scout.*
WALSH, *a superintendent of the NWMP in charge of Fort Walsh.*
MRS. ANDERSON, *a settler.*
CROW EAGLE, *a Cree.*
McCUTCHEON, *a sergeant in the NWMP.*
MARY, *wife of Major Walsh.*
SITTING BULL, *a chief of the Hunkpapa Sioux.*
PRETTY PLUME, *wife of Sitting Bull.*
CROWFOOT, *son of Sitting Bull.*
GALL, *a chief of the Hunkpapa Sioux.*
WHITE DOG, *an Assiniboine.*
TERRY, *a general in the U.S. Army.*
COLONEL MacLEOD, *commissioner of the NWMP.*

Detachment @ Klondike 1898

Prologue − *The Present*

*The characters in the prologue become the characters in the
play proper. McCUTCHEON plays IAN, the bartender.
SITTING BULL is the PROSPECTOR; CROW
EAGLE is BILLY, the harmonica player in the saloon.
LOUIS and MacLEOD are a couple of poker players.
CROWFOOT is JOEIE, the newspaper boy. JENNIE
is MRS. ANDERSON. WALSH and HARRY play
themselves. WALSH is in civvies, impeccably dressed,
in contrast to the other characters who look dirty and
disreputable. The atmosphere in the prologue is smoky, as
if the scene were lit by a coal-oil lamp with a dirty
chimney.*

*The scene is from WALSH's point of view, and the
freezes are momentary arrests in the action and are broken
by the character's speech or action following. The
impression given is similar to that experienced when one
is drunk or under great mental stress. CLARENCE* concurrel
*stands outside of the prologue scene, never taking his eyes
off WALSH. He has on his red tunic and he exists
only in WALSH's mind. He is not part of the prologue
scene and his scream is heard only by WALSH.*

*There is no break in staging between the prologue and
Act One.*

9

sound effects

The sound of wind is heard — a mournful sound. In a very dim light, the characters suddenly appear on the periphery of the playing area. WALSH is not among them. They freeze there for a moment, and then, quickly and silently, like ghosts, take their positions onstage, with the exception of HARRY, JOEIE and CLARENCE, who remain in the shadows. The characters freeze on stage, all facing WALSH's entrance. There is an increase in the howling of the wind and WALSH appears in a spotlight somewhat brighter than the general dim lighting. The wind fades as WALSH enters. He is walking very slowly and carefully, as if he were the tiniest bit drunk. As he enters, JENNIE pulls out a chair at a table and IAN pours a drink into a glass on the table. The PROSPECTOR is blocking WALSH's way and WALSH stops. The PROSPECTOR steps aside and WALSH continues toward the table. All the characters watch him. WALSH stops at the chair, looks out at CLARENCE and turns the chair so that he no longer faces CLARENCE. He sits. There is a momentary freeze, then WALSH reaches for his drink, breaking the freeze. BILLY begins playing the harmonica; JENNIE begins to sing and to move among the characters, tipping a hat here and rubbing an arm there as she passes. The characters come alive and the light brightens a bit so that WALSH's spotlight is gone — although the light is still not full.

JENNIE: *singing*
George Carmack on Bonanza Creek went out to look
    for gold,
I wonder why, I wonder why.
Oldtimers said it was no use, the water was too cold.
I wonder why, I wonder why.

PROSPECTOR:
Another verse, Jennie!

JENNIE:
Is there somethin' else you'd have me do, Mr. Walsh?

10

WALSH:
    Do you know . . . "Break the News to Mother"?

JENNIE:
    There's not much I don't know. How the hell did you
    think I ended up in Dawson?

        Laughs and guffaws are heard from the boys.

WALSH:
    I always liked "Break the News to Mother."

JENNIE: *singing*
    I wonder why, I wonder why.

HARRY: *entering from the shadows*
    Jeeeesus Chriiiist! It's colder than a witch's diddy.

        *All the characters turn and look at him, with the
        exception of WALSH.*

    How about some eats here?

JENNIE:
    Girls, upstairs to the left; a drink, we can give you
    here.

BILLY:
    But you can't buy what there ain't none of. . . .

PROSPECTOR:
    Which is grub.

        *There is a momentary freeze which affects everyone but
        WALSH, who looks at HARRY.*

JENNIE: *singing as BILLY plays the harmonica*
    They said that he might search the creek until the
        world did end,
    But not enough of gold he'd find a postage stamp
        to send—

11

*JENNIE stops singing abruptly as HARRY pulls out
his poke. There is a momentary freeze. It affects everyone
but WALSH. The freeze is broken by hoarse whispers.*

BILLY:
Better put away that poke, mister.

PROSPECTOR:
We got a grafter in the room.   *one who makes*
                                    gain — bribe

He indicates WALSH.

Ain't you noticed?

JENNIE:
He'd as soon take ten percent off the top of that as
look at you.

WALSH: *raising his glass to them*
Gentlemen — and sweet Jennie.

BILLY: *in a low voice*
To hell with Mr. Walsh.

*There is a momentary freeze as they all watch WALSH
drink. The freeze is broken by WALSH when he puts
down his glass. IAN moves to fill it. BILLY begins
playing "Garryowen" on his harmonica.*

HARRY:
Where'd you hear that song? You a Yankee fella?
You a cavalry man?

BILLY:
Don't have to be a cavalry man to know a song,
mister.

He resumes playing his harmonica.

12

JENNIE:
Here's a lady done a lot of ridin' and she don't know that song.

PROSPECTOR:
"Garryowen."

WALSH knocks over his drink. There is a momentary freeze as they all look at WALSH and he stares at his spilled drink.

JENNIE:
Ah, Mr. Walsh, you've spilled your drink. A drink for Mr. Walsh.

IAN rights his glass and pours him another drink.

BILLY:
To hell with Mr. Walsh.

He resumes playing his harmonica and "Garryowen" builds with the sound of a military band creeping in and growing in volume.

HARRY:
"Garryowen." Marching song of the 7th Cavalry.   ↙
Custer's outfit.

JENNIE:
Who's that?

HARRY:
A long hair killed with long knives at the Greasy Grass.

JENNIE:
We speak English here, mister.

"Garryowen" stops abruptly. WALSH bangs down his glass. There is another freeze as he looks around slowly and speaks clearly, carefully, announcing it, giving the

impression once again of perhaps being drunk, but really being completely under control.

WALSH:

General George Armstrong Custer . . . killed with 261 men of the 7th Cavalry of the United States Army . . . at the Little Big Horn, Montana, June 25th, 1876.

There is a pause. The freeze is broken as he picks up his drink. BILLY begins playing a ragtime tune on his harmonica. The lights brighten. The characters resume their talk.

HARRY:

Who's your grafter?

IAN:

That's Major Walsh — but he's not with the force. He's Commissioner of the Yukon now.

JENNIE:

Did you see me front? Not a bit of snow to the street. Walsh may not be with the force, but he gets a good day's work out of 'em.

She laughs.

I must be the only whorehouse in the north whose front is shovelled clear by the North West Mounted on the orders of the Commissioner of the Yukon.

They all look at WALSH.

He knows what those boys are good for.

JOEIE: *moving out of the shadows*
Anyone want to buy a paper?

JENNIE:
    Hey, Joeie's here with the *Nugget.* . . . Pass the hat
round for Joeie! Isn't he a dear?

    The PROSPECTOR starts around with the hat for
    JOEIE. JENNIE puts her arm around JOEIE.

    His Da froze and his Mum takes in washin'. He's
sweet Jennie's dear, aren't you, Joeie? You're sweet
Jennie's sweetheart, aren't you?

    The PROSPECTOR approaches WALSH after
    collecting some money from the others.

PROSPECTOR: *holding out the hat*
    For Joeie.

    WALSH looks at him. There is a look of
    incomprehension in his gaze.

    I'm askin' for somethin' for the little boy.

WALSH:
    I can give you nothing.

PROSPECTOR:
    You and your kind have taken enough off us. You
kin spare somethin' for the little boy.

WALSH:
    I can give you nothing!

PROSPECTOR:
    It ain't enough you're a son-of-a-bitch, you gotta be a
cheap son-of-a-bitch!

    WALSH hits him in the face, knocking him down. As
    he goes to get up, he plants a foot in his back, sending
    him sprawling.

CLARENCE: *screaming from the shadows*
Noooooooo!

> *There is a freeze with WALSH with his hand upraised to hit the PROSPECTOR; IAN with the bottle raised as a club; JENNIE drawing JOEIE to her. All of the characters in the saloon are in positions of action, except for HARRY who is a spectator. There is a pause, then HARRY sets forward, moving among the frozen characters.*

HARRY: *addressing the audience*
The Klondike! 1898! And the end for Major James A. Walsh, formerly of the North West Mounted Police, an original member of the first contingent of that force, formed in 1873 by Sir John A. MacDonald to police the Canadian West!

> *He smashes his fist on the table. The freeze ends. HARRY continues as the actors leave.*

Major Walsh never met General Custer, which was kinda a pity, 'cause the day Custer met Sittin' Bull was the beginning of the end for Major Walsh. . . . Old Glory Hound Custer — now he had a fail-proof plan for killin' off Injuns. First off, you found yourself some friendlies. You was forced to kill friendlies 'cause it was too difficult findin' hostiles, but friendlies camped near the forts, to show their goodwill kinda like, and it weren't too hard to come across a bunch of 'em set up in some cozy little hollow, flyin' the 'merican flag for good measure.

> *He laughs a dry chuckle.*

Well now, once you picked yourself some Injuns, you gotta pick yourself a time. Custer thought winter was the best, for the Injun had always figured fightin' in winter wasn't sportin' like, and avoided it if he could. . . . Custer was an early riser — and if you team up a winter date with a 4 a.m. charge, when the

Injuns was all asleep, you pretty well had it made.... Course, tactics comes into it. Custer did all right there too. 'Member that cozy little hollow I mentioned? Sorta a tube-like hollow was best, 'cause what you did was send a bunch of men in one end of the tube and, of course, all hell broke loose there, what with kids screamin', women runnin' and men lookin' for somethin' to hit back with, and the whole works naked as the day they was born, it bein' the middle of the night as far as they was concerned. Anyway, as their attention was somewhat di-verted by this here attack at one end of the tube, Custer, with a bunch of the boys, would sneak round t' other end and ride through, hell-bent for whoop-up, killin' off the strays, and generally gettin' a lot of 'em in the back while they was lookin' t' other way....
It were a pretty efficient way to fight a war.... The flag did its bit too, for the Injuns was prone to rally under it, thinkin' maybe the fact they was friendly had been missed; occasionally one of 'em even had time to run up a white flag.

He reminisces.

There was almost a kinda festive at-mos-phere to a Custer attack, what with his marchin' band playing "Garryowen." Custer liked to charge to music, and "Garryowen" was his favourite, although he was fond of "The Girl I Left Behind" too.... Still, generally, it was "Garryowen."

He whistles a few bars of "Garryowen." The tune begins brightly, but becomes slower and slower, then stops. There is silence for a second. He continues speaking — not as lightly as in the first part of his monologue.

The Little Big Horn... June 25th... 1876. ...
First off, wrong time! June ain't December — and that's a fact. Just shows how success kin go to your head. And the Injuns at the Little Big Horn weren't friendly. They was hostile. They was hostile as hell.

17

Sittin' Bull and the Sioux had listened to the 'merican government say, "The utmost good faith shall always be observed towards the Indians, and their land and property shall never be taken from them without their consent." They had taken the government at its word — bein' savages, they weren't too familiar with governments and all, so it was an understandable mistake. . . . So, we got wrong month, and wrong bunch of Injuns. These Sioux weren't sittin' under no flag waitin' to be popped off like passenger pigeons. . . . On June 25th, Custer was up at 4 a.m. all right. Trouble was he never found no Injuns till noon time. His fail-proof plan for killin' off Injuns was goin' to hell in a hand basket. On top of everythin' else, the marchin' band had a prior engagement with General Terry. . . . So, here's Custer . . . at noon time . . . in late June . . . with no marchin' band . . . comin' upon a camp of hostiles. Well now, it weren't hardly a camp either. It was a gathering together, under Sittin' Bull, of the last of those Injuns who weren't willin' to swap their huntin' grounds and freedom for a small corner of a reservation, 'bout 4,000 warriors, plus women and children. And what they was camped in wasn't, by no stretch of the imagination, a tube-like hollow. It was a gentle rollin' sweep of Montana prairie. . . . Custer, seein' it was gettin' later in the day by the minute, and probably wantin' to avoid that early afternoon slump most early risers suffer from, decided to attack without sendin' out a scout to see how far this here camp of Injuns extended. He had 'bout 500 men, and he figured that would be enough with some left over. . . . "Take no prisoners" was the order. . . . Major Reno, who, incidentally, had never fought Injuns before, only other 'mericans in the Civil War . . . this here Reno was given the honour of ridin' with 'bout half the men into one end of the non-tube. Which he did. And got the bejesus beat out of him. He made a hasty retreat to a bluff where he sat with his men for two days, cursin' Custer for runnin' off and leavin' them to the mercy of the Injuns and the sun. Forgot to mention that Custer did have this

unfortunate habit of cuttin' his losses and ridin'
off. . . . This time, Custer hadn't ridden off. He wasn't
goin' nowhere. He had taken his half of the 7th,
ridden a couple of miles, and cut down to what he
figured was the outskirts of the camp. Two miles. His
figurin' was 'bout eight miles out. He found Injuns
aplenty — and none of them was facin' the other
way. . . . On June 28th, General Terry came on a
yellow-brown slope dotted with dead horses and pale
white bodies — the dead — stripped of arms,
ammunition, equipment . . . and clothin'. . . . At the
summit of the slope stood a horse. The sole survivor
of Custer's Last Stand was a clay-coloured
horse — Comanche — still on his feet with ten bullet
holes in him. The bullet holes eventually healed and
on April 10th, 1878, the horse was commissioned
"second commandin' officer" of the 7th
Cavalry . . . and, on all occasions of ceremony,
saddled, bridled, draped in mournin' and led by a
mounted trooper, Comanche paraded with the
regiment. . . . I hear tell, that when Terry looked on
Custer's dead body, he wept, and said, "The flower of
the American Army is gone." . . . Well now, the rest
of the 'merican Army was out to avenge the "Custer
Massacre." Sittin' Bull and the Sioux were hard to lay
hands on, but there was always the friendlies.

Act One

The action continues without a break.

[handwritten: The Past by Action moved (scenes) Harry]

HARRY: *beginning to move treaty goods*
Across the line, in the country of the Great White
Mother, Major James A. Walsh of the North West
Mounted was enforcin' law and order as decreed by
Her Majesty's Government.

CLARENCE: *offstage*
Hey, Harry!

HARRY:
I had . . . what you might call, vacated the U-nited
States and had myself a job as wagon master. . . .

CLARENCE: *offstage*
Harry! What're you doin'? Come on!

HARRY:
I'm comin'! I was running treaty goods for Canadian
Injuns into Fort Walsh.

CLARENCE: *offstage*
Jesus Christ, Harry! Would you give me a hand!

HARRY: *without moving to go*
I said, I'm comin'!

CLARENCE:
Never mind, you lazy bastard!

Grunts and groans of effort are heard.

I'll do it myself!

HARRY:
Be right with you.

CLARENCE enters, bent double under a packing case. HARRY sits and watches him.

Hey, you better watch out for . . .

CLARENCE trips over a ploughshare. He falls flat on his face, spilling the packing case which is full of shovels.

. . . the ploughshare.

CLARENCE sits up, looking around at the shovels, the packing case.

CLARENCE: *speaking plaintively*
What the hell are they goin' to do with these?

HARRY: *matter-of-factly*
Nothin'.

CLARENCE:
What do you mean, nothin'?

HARRY: *explaining a fact of life*
They're gonna do nothin' with these. We're gonna haul 'em all over here, your Major's gonna pass 'em all out and they're gonna haul 'em all away. And they

Ploughshare

ain't gonna do nothin' with 'em. The seed's gonna rot, the 'shares gonna rust and them goddamn shovels is just gonna lie where they flung 'em.

CLARENCE:
If they aren't gonna use 'em, why're we luggin' them around?

HARRY:
I'll tell you somethin', your Major's gonna be madder than a wet hen when he sees this lot. Second lot I brung in this month. First lot, the Major, he threw a real fit, said he was gonna write the Prime Minister, tell 'im to stuff his farm u-tensils.

CLARENCE:
Hey, did you hear the talk over at the fort?

HARRY bites off a chaw of tobacco and looks at CLARENCE disdainfully.

HARRY:
That talk's everywhere, Clarence.

CLARENCE:
Do you believe it?

HARRY:
Don't see why it couldn't be true.

CLARENCE:
Aren't you scared?

HARRY:
Now, why'd I be scared, Clarence?

CLARENCE:
We're gonna have ourselves an Injun War, just like the States, that's why!

HARRY gives him a dry look.

CLARENCE:
> The Sioux are headed north. . . . An Injun War! . . . I could get to kill the man who killed Custer!

HARRY:
> And who might that be?

CLARENCE:
> Why, Sittin' Bull, of course.

HARRY:
> How'd you know it was him personally killed Custer?

CLARENCE: *defensively*
> Well . . . everybody says so! It was Sittin' Bull himself killed Custer at the Little Big Horn — with his huntin' knife!

> *He thinks about it and backs down a bit.*

> I guess the only ones know for sure are the men who died with Custer, eh?

HARRY: *politely*
> Ain't you forgettin' somethin'?

CLARENCE:
> What?

HARRY:
> I seem to recollect there was some other people present at the event.

CLARENCE:
> Who?

HARRY:
> Jesus Christ, Clarence! The Indians, that's who! You think a white man's the only person kin know anythin' for sure! Whyn't you try askin' an Injun who killed Custer? You bleedin' redcoats don't know nothin'!

24

CLARENCE: *insulted*
 You wanna fight?

> *HARRY looks at CLARENCE and directs a spittle*
> *of tobacco juice at CLARENCE's feet.*
> *CLARENCE hauls back his fist.*

LOUIS: *from the shadows, speaking to CLARENCE*
 'Ey!

> *WALSH enters, his attention fixed on the crates.*

WALSH:
 What the hell's this?

HARRY: *clearing his throat*
 Well, sir, I 'spect you'd say . . . it was more. . . .

WALSH:
 And this . . . and this . . . and this!

> *He slaps each item with his riding crop.*

LOUIS: *attempting to be helpful*
 'Dat's ploughshare. We got 'em last time.

WALSH:
 I know we got them last time. Why're we getting them
 this time?

> *LOUIS shrugs. WALSH's glance falls on*
> *CLARENCE. He notices him for the first time.*
> *CLARENCE feels obliged to say something.*

CLARENCE:
 I . . . I don't know, sir.

> *WALSH's irritation seems to go and his manner*
> *changes.*

CLARENCE:
    Yes, sir.

WALSH:
    Name?

CLARENCE:
    Constable Clarence Underhill, sir!

WALSH:
    Welcome to the fort, Constable. Keep your eyes, ears
    and mind open . . .

CLARENCE:
    Yes, s . . . .

WALSH:
    . . . and your mouth shut.

        He turns to HARRY and speaks real friendly.

    All right, Harry.

        He leans on a crate beside HARRY.

    What is all this?

        He indicates the implements with his riding crop.

HARRY:
    Well, sir. . . .

WALSH: *exceedingly friendly*
    Some immigrant family ordered it, I suppose. . . .

HARRY:
    Ah . . . I can't rightly say that, sir.

WALSH:
    Aha. . . . Then you're taking it up to Calgary, are you,
    for some poor witless farmer there?

HARRY:
No, sir. . . . Not that either.

WALSH:
Mmmm. . . . Planning on homesteading yourself, are you?

HARRY smiles. The idea amuses him.

HARRY:
Not very likely, sir.

WALSH stares at HARRY for a second. He lowers his voice and his speech builds.

WALSH:
Are you telling me, man, that once again the government has seen fit to burden me and the natives of these parts with another load of seed and equipment to rot and rust when they know goddamn well, because I've told them time and again, that these Indians are not, and will never be, farmers!

There is a pause as WALSH stares at HARRY.

HARRY: *answering weakly*
That's it, sir.

WALSH:
Right!

His anger seems to subside.

Well . . . can't be helped, can it?

He walks around one of the crates, tapping it with his riding crop, then he barks.

Bill of lading!

He extends his hand.

CLARENCE: *startled*
    Ah! Yes, sir!

> *He feels in his pocket as WALSH watches him
> expressionless. He finds the bill, presents it to
> WALSH—but not quite in his hand. The bill begins to
> float to the ground. He retrieves it and places it in
> WALSH's hand.*

WALSH: *dryly*
    Thank you, Constable.

CLARENCE:
    Yes, sir!

> *WALSH looks at CLARENCE, then moves away with
> HARRY.*

WALSH:
    What have you got there, Harry?

> *He and HARRY begin to check the number of crates.
> LOUIS looks over to CLARENCE.*

LOUIS:
    'Ey . . . 'ey dere. . . .

> *He beckons him with his finger. CLARENCE moves
> over to him, although he's still more or less at attention
> and focused on WALSH in case he should suddenly want
> something.*

Dis . . . a . . . first time you meet da . . .

> *He nods towards WALSH.*

. . . commandin' officer up close, eh?

> *CLARENCE nods and looks at LOUIS warily.*

LOUIS looks somewhat disreputable in his scout outfit.

What you think of 'im?

CLARENCE:
He seems a little. . . .

He casts a nervous clance at WALSH.

WALSH: *to HARRY*
Read it yourself!

He thrusts the bill at HARRY.

What does that look like to you?

CLARENCE smiles weakly at LOUIS, who smiles back.

HARRY:
It . . . ah . . . looks like we're missin' one crate, Major.

WALSH:
I trust you'll find it.

HARRY:
I'll do that . . . yes, I will, Major. First thing I hit Fort MacLeod.

WALSH:
Right.

He takes the bill and begins to check it against the goods listed on the outside of the crates.

So . . . contents. . . .

HARRY assists him.

LOUIS: *indicating himself*
Louis Leveille.

He shakes hands with CLARENCE.

CLARENCE:
Fort Walsh scout. . . . Mother red, father white . . . but not so white as da Major dere. . . . Louis' father, French.

> *He laughs. CLARENCE realizes it's a joke and smiles back.*

WALSH:
Mark it off! Mark it off!

> *HARRY does so. CLARENCE glances at them nervously.*

LOUIS:
Ah . . . don't worry . . . mean nothin'. . . . Just 'is way. He care a lot and so he yell a lot, eh?

CLARENCE:
Yeah. I guess you gotta know a lot to be an officer.

LOUIS:
Louis tell yuh somethin'. . . . Take all da books, da news dat da white man prints, take all dat Bible book, take all dose things you learn from . . . lay dem on da prairie . . . and da sun . . . da rain . . . da snow . . . pouf! You wanna learn, you study inside here . . .

> *He taps his head.*

. . . and here . . .

> *He taps his chest.*

. . . and how it is wit' you and me . . .

> *He indicates the two of them.*

... and how it is wit' you and all....

He indicates the surroundings.

Travel 'round da Medicine Wheel. Den you know ⸜
somethin'.

WALSH: *approaching LOUIS and CLARENCE*
Well, Louis, there's another lot, courtesy of those
fools in Ottawa.

LOUIS:
Dose fools that're sittin' dere ain't such fools as da
people dat sent dem dere, eh, Major?

*WALSH chuckles. HARRY begins to clear away
the treaty goods.*

MRS. ANDERSON: *offstage*
Major Walsh! Oh, Major!

*WALSH sighs. MRS. ANDERSON enters almost
hysterical.*

Major Walsh!

WALSH: *smiling at MRS. ANDERSON*
Yes, Mrs. Anderson.

MRS. ANDERSON: *almost in tears*
Major Walsh, the most terrible thing has happened.

*CROW EAGLE enters with great dignity. He
walks a bit ahead of Sergeant McCUTCHEON.
He is in custody, although there is no hand on him.*

WALSH:
Now, it's all right, Mrs. Anderson. Just tell us what
this is all about.

MRS. ANDERSON:
Ah, Major . . . this savage . . . this heathen . . . this . . .
Indian has stolen my washtub!

A pained expression passes over WALSH's face.
He shakes his head and makes an almost inaudible
tut-tut sound.

Yes! It was right outside the door and these heathens
snuck up and stole it! I'm counting on you, Major, to
return that tub! I mean, what am I to rinse in otherwise?

WALSH:
Well, Crow Eagle, did you take this white lady's tub?

CROW EAGLE:
That is so.

MRS. ANDERSON:
What did I tell you?

She circles CROW EAGLE in a rage.

Mark my words, they'll be killing us in our sleep
next!

WALSH: *placating her*
Mrs. Anderson. . . .

He turns to CROW EAGLE.

Why'd you take the tub?

CROW EAGLE:
We needed a drum.

WALSH:
The Great White Mother'd be very angry if she
discovered you'd taken this white lady's washtub.

CROW EAGLE:
> I am sure if the Great White Mother knew how much we needed that drum, she would be glad to let us keep it.

MRS. ANDERSON:
> As if the Queen cared about them!

CROW EAGLE:
> We have cut the bottom out of that tub and covered it with buffalo skin. It makes a very good drum.

LOUIS:
> Da white lady has 'nother tub ... why does she not use dat?

> *MRS. ANDERSON goes to seize CROW EAGLE's arm.*

MRS. ANDERSON:
> What's mine's my own! You'll not take. . . .

> *WALSH takes her arm and draws her aside.*

WALSH:
> Mrs. Anderson!

MRS. ANDERSON:
> Whose side are you on, Jim?

WALSH:
> I was unaware we were choosing sides. My job is to keep the peace and see that justice is done.

MRS. ANDERSON:
> Then get me my tub!

WALSH: *a trifle tired*
> Louis, explain it to him.

LOUIS: *explaining to CROW EAGLE in Cree*
Na-mo-ya ta-ki otin-a-man ki-kwhy a-ka a-tipay-
hitaman (It is not lawful to take what is not your
own). . . .

CROW EAGLE: *dismissing LOUIS and speaking directly to*
WALSH White Forehead Chief! Why we should not
keep it?

WALSH: *after a pause*
You must not take articles from the whites again.
They need even what they appear not to need. . . .
And you must bring skins in payment for the . . .
drum. . . . Make sure he understands, Louis.

LOUIS draws CROW EAGLE aside and speaks to
him in muffled conversation while WALSH continues
with MRS. ANDERSON.

LOUIS:
Wapi-ka-tik-oki-maw it-o-wew-may-scootch ata-yuk
ta-pa-so-wa-chik to tippo-what misti-kwa-shihk-asa
kotin-nut (The White Forehead Chief says you must
bring skins in payment for the drum you have taken).

CROW EAGLE:
Ni-ka-to-tayn namaya-ni-nistotayn ma-ka ni-ka-to-
tayn keespin Wapi-ka-tik ekosi it-o-wew-ni-ka-to-tayn
(I will do it. I do not understand it, but I will do it. If
the White Forehead Chief says it . . . I will do it).

LOUIS:
Pi-ko ta-na-hi-ta-wat Okimaskoew Kwa-yask ta-pa-
mi-hayew ki-ta-yis-si-ni-ma apo tchi ke-yom ta-wan-
kiski-sew kiya (You must obey the Great White
Mother's law. She will look after your people if you
do. Otherwise, she will forget you).

CROW EAGLE:

> Wapi-ka-tik chee pa-taw aso-ta-ma-to-aina paski-si-gana, mosiniya nin-ta wahitaynan paskowaw mastosak aya-wak sa-ka-staynok (Has she sent the White Forehead Chief the goods that I asked for my people? We need ammunition, we have seen buffalo to the south).

WALSH: *steering MRS. ANDERSON away*

> Now, look, Emma....

MRS. ANDERSON:

> What about my tub?

WALSH:

> Emma... the Indians, they see two tubs in your yard.... You have to remember they've a different background from us....

MRS. ANDERSON:

> Background? They don't have any background.

WALSH:

> Well, as I was saying....

MRS. ANDERSON:

> Are you telling me I'm not getting my tub back?

WALSH:

> That's right, Emma.

MRS. ANDERSON:

> What will you do when they murder us in our beds? You're nothing but a....

WALSH:

> Would you have me throw him in chains? To hell with your damed old tub! We're not going to start an Indian War over it!

MRS. ANDERSON:
> No! You'll sit by and let the Sioux do that!

> *She whirls around and exits. WALSH stands stiff
> and tense as she exits, then he relaxes and turns to
> McCUTCHEON. He smiles, sighs and shakes
> his head.*

WALSH:
> The Sioux?... Well, McCutcheon... hell hath no
> fury like a woman deprived of her washtub.

> *He walks around the equipment, looking at it
> casually.*

> You'd think it was her very existence.

McCUTCHEON:
> Aye, sir. You're right there. I tell ye, I'd rather face a
> hostile in a fit of pique than Mrs. Anderson with her
> dander up....

LOUIS:
> Crow Eagle asks for ammunition to hunt da buffalo.
> His scouts have seen a small herd to da south.

WALSH:
> Every year there're fewer buffalo and soon there will
> be no more. His people must think of next year and
> the year after.

LOUIS: *almost gently*
> Ever since he was born, he has eaten wild meat. His
> father and his grandfather ate wild meat. He cannot
> give up quickly the customs of his fathers.

> *WALSH speaks directly to CROW EAGLE.*

36

WALSH: *speaking formally*
When the white man comes, the buffalo goes.... And with the buffalo goes the life you have known. You cannot stop this happening anymore than you can stop the sun or the moon. You must find a new life.... That is why the Great White Mother sends you these ...

He indicates the implements.

... so you can start a new life.

CROW EAGLE:
I do not wish to be servant to a cow.

HARRY: *laughing*
He's got somethin' there....

WALSH:
Yes, well... McCutcheon, take him over to the post and see he gets ammunition for the hunt.

McCUTCHEON:
Aye, sir.

He and CROW EAGLE go to leave.

WALSH:
Crow Eagle, you must think of the time when there are no more buffalo.

CROW EAGLE:
When there are no more buffalo ... there are no more Indians.

He and McCUTCHEON exit. WALSH watches them leave.

WALSH: *to himself*
I ask you, can you see that man bent double over a hoe?

HARRY:
Don't appear likely they'll ever be farmers, that's a fact.

WALSH:
Farmers? Not farmers! If they're to grow anything in this dust bowl, the government'll have to turn them into magicians!

CLARENCE: *standing at attention*
Excuse me, sir... permission to speak, sir.

WALSH appears lost in his thoughts as he stares after CROW EAGLE.

WALSH:
Yes... what is it?

CLARENCE:
There's been some talk, sir, among the men at the post... about the hostiles from the States.

WALSH: *still not particularly attentive*
Go on....

CLARENCE: *encouraged*
About them comin' up into Canada.... Sittin' Bull and the whole Sioux nation comin' up into Canada to get away from the U.S. Army....

Sometime during CLARENCE's speech, WALSH becomes alert and is listening.

WALSH:
Yes?

CLARENCE:
Well... I was just wonderin', sir, if that was true... I mean, the whole Sioux nation, sir? And we only got 'bout 60 men here...

WALSH:
 Yes.

CLARENCE:
 . . . and you know . . . I'm not askin' for myself, sir,
 it's just that I'd like to write a last letter home to me
 Mum if we . . . if we were on the verge of war, sir, or
 anything like that . . . sir.

WALSH: *speaking quietly*
 What have the Sioux done?

CLARENCE: *blurting it out*
 They killed Custer!

WALSH:
 And Custer killed them.

CLARENCE:
 Yes, sir.

WALSH:
 What have the Sioux done to us?

> *CLARENCE looks nervously at HARRY, then
> back to WALSH.*

CLARENCE:
 Nothin', sir?

WALSH:
 In which case, I don't believe we're on the verge of
 war with them.

> *He turns to LOUIS and speaks to him lightly.*

What do you say, Louis?

LOUIS: *smiling*
I think our redcoats too damn busy chasin' 'merican whiskey traders. Dey much worse trouble dan any Sioux I run across.

WALSH: *smiling*
My sentiments exactly.

He and LOUIS start off. The sound of the arrival of the Sioux creeps in very softly — muted voices, horses, faint drums and singing. It can bearly be heard.

CLARENCE:
Sir!

WALSH: *turning back to him*
Yes, Constable?

CLARENCE: *speaking quickly*
Request permission to accompany the Major when he rides out to meet Sittin' Bull and the Sioux, sir!

WALSH:
What about that letter to your mother?

CLARENCE:
I'll write it tonight, sir.

WALSH has a hard time keeping a smile off his face.

WALSH:
Permission granted.

WALSH exits as CLARENCE and HARRY watch him. CLARENCE is tense and HARRY is casual, then CLARENCE looks at HARRY, relaxes, grins and leaps into the air, throwing his hat off. There is a certain similarity to an Indian youth after his first coup.

CLARENCE:
Yip yip yip yip yipeeeeeeeeeeeeeeee! Whahooo!

> *CLARENCE and HARRY exit. The lights dim as LOUIS crouches, listening to the sound of the Sioux arriving which builds. LOUIS moves about as if he were watching the arrival of the Sioux. The sound is well established before he speaks.*

LOUIS:
Tabernacle!

> *He casts a glance over his shoulder.*

Major! Dis way!

> *WALSH and McCUTCHEON enter. They stand on a slight rise.*

See . . . da village is dere.

> *He points in one direction.*

Dat dust, dat is more joinin' dose already camped.

> *WALSH hands his binoculars to McCUTCHEON. He gazes at the village, using only his naked eye, as the scout does.*

WALSH:
Must be . . . what . . . two miles away? What would you say, Louis?

LOUIS: *smiling*
Louis say you damn good pupil.

WALSH: *smiling*
Louis damn good teacher.

McCUTCHEON: *looking through the binoculars, then lowering them* Must be 2,000 people there.

LOUIS:
Maybe so. . . . 5,000.

CLARENCE enters.

CLARENCE:
The horses're picketed, sir.

WALSH turns to CLARENCE and speaks to him with an intensity that indicates he is taut as a bow string and ready for anything.

WALSH:
You wanted to see the Sioux, Constable. . . all right, here they come. I want you to remember something. . . . You do not draw your gun unless you see me draw mine. You will follow orders exactly, precisely and immediately. If you do one thing that precipitates trouble between us and the Sioux, you need not worry about a redskin taking your scalp. I myself will place a bullet between your eyes faster than you can say write-a-letter-home.

It is a threat he means.

Do you understand?

For the first time, CLARENCE is aware of the potential explosiveness of the situation.

CLARENCE:
I do, sir.

The sound is building.

WALSH:
Louis, beside me. . . . McCutcheon and Underhill, behind. . . .

They take up their positions. WALSH gives a quick look to CLARENCE.

I rely on you to uphold the honour of the force.

*The sound is at its crescendo — all around the
audience — for several seconds. The sound stops.
There is a pause.*

*GALL enters. He is followed by SITTING BULL,
who looks austere. He has one feather
in his hair. They stop a short distance from WALSH.
WALSH raises his hand, palm outward. GALL returns
the gesture. There is silence for a second.*

Louis, tell them. . . .

GALL:
We speak as men — to each other.

He means that they do not need an interpreter.

I am Gall of the Hunkpapa Lakota.

WALSH:
You've crossed the line into the country of the Great
White Mother.

*GALL stares at WALSH impassively. SITTING
BULL follows their conversation. His movements,
if any, are slow and deliberate. He is a man of
great presence and personal magnetism. It is not
necessary for him to speak or to draw attention to
himself in any way for one to be aware of his
strength of character. It is his custom to carefully
size up a situation before committing himself to a
course of action.*

I am a soldier of the Great White Mother. You may
know me, and others like me, by my red coat.

He indicates his tunic.

GALL: *offering WALSH a George III medal*
My grandfather was a soldier for the grandfather of
Queen Victoria. At that time, your people told him
that the Sioux nation belonged to that grandfather of
the Queen. My people fought against the Longknives
for your people then. We were told that you would
always look after your red children. Now the
Longknives have stolen our land. We have no place
to go. We come home to you asking for that
protection you promised.

> *WALSH takes the medal from GALL and examines
> it. He looks at GALL. He is not actually prepared
> for this specific argument about Canada's obligation
> to the Sioux.*

McCUTCHEON: *speaking quietly*
What is it, sir?

> *WALSH passes the medal to McCUTCHEON.*

WALSH:
It's a George III medal. The Sioux fought for the
British in 1776 against the Americans.

> *He looks at GALL and speaks carefully. His
> orders from Ottawa have not covered this exigency.*

We are your friends, that is true. . . .

GALL:
The Lakota has need of friends. I want you to know
this trouble was not begun by us. The Longknives
have come out of the night and for campfires they
have lit our lodges. Our women weep and the nostrils
of our babies must be pinched lest they cry out and
give us away. At the Greasy Grass, the Long Hair
attacked our camp and we rose up like the buffalo
bull when the cows are attacked and we rubbed him
out. Now we are hunted as we hunt animals . . . and
we have crossed the line.

44

LOUIS: *nudging WALSH*
>'Ey . . . on the ridge . . . is dat not da horse of Père de Corbay?

>*WALSH looks, frowns, then indicates the hills.*

WALSH:
>Whose horses graze there?

GALL: *looking at the hills*
>White Dog's, our Assiniboine brother.

WALSH:
>I wish to speak to him.

>>*The sound of rattles and drums are heard. GALL exits. CLARENCE shifts from side to side nervously. McCUTCHEON gives him a look.*

McCUTCHEON: *in a low voice*
>Easy, laddie.

CLARENCE: *taking a slow look over his shoulder*
>We're bloody well surrounded, Sergeant.

McCUTCHEON:
>Never ye mind, laddie. Just keep your eye on the Major.

>>*WALSH takes a slow walk. He whistles, then he stops, looking directly at SITTING BULL.*

WALSH:
>Gall!

>>*GALL turns toward him.*

>I ask the name of the man who stands with us.

GALL:
>A wise man. . . .

WHITE DOG enters. He carries a rifle in one hand.

WALSH: *speaking quickly*
McCutcheon!

WHITE DOG: *belligerently*
White Dog.

WALSH:
The horses on the ridge, are they yours?

WHITE DOG: *antagonistically*
You say!

WALSH: *snapping at McCUTCHEON*
McCutcheon!

> *McCUTCHEON moves quickly and seizes
> WHITE DOG's arms. WHITE DOG resists, but
> McCUTCHEON holds him immobile. WALSH's hand
> rests easily, almost casually, on his holstered gun. As
> McCUTCHEON seizes WHITE DOG, he cries out.
> There is a swelling of sound from the surrounding Sioux.
> WALSH raises his voice and announces as the sound
> continues in the background.*

Those are the horses of Père de Corbay! His brand
can be seen from here! White Dog is under arrest for
stealing!

WHITE DOG:
I find loose! It is custom, horses taken! No law!

WALSH: *after a pause*
Release him!

> *McCUTCHEON releases him.*

Next time, you find horses not belonging to you, they
must be left alone!

WHITE DOG: *as he turns to leave, calling back threateningly*
Meet again, Wichitas!

WALSH:
White Dog!

> *He walks up to WHITE DOG, oblivious of his rifle.*

Repeat your words.

WHITE DOG: *a coward*
Meet again sometime.

WALSH: *speaking quietly, but not without menace*
Take back those words.

> *WHITE DOG hestitates a minute, then looks to SITTING BULL and back at WALSH.*

WHITE DOG:
White Dog not threaten.

WALSH: *inclining his head slightly*
Then go. I have no grudge against White Dog.

> *WHITE DOG hurries off. The background sound swells. WALSH walks over to SITTING BULL, who raises his hand. The noise stops.*

SITTING BULL:
These people are my people. I am Sitting Bull.

WALSH:
Major James Walsh of the North West Mounted Police.

> *He extends his hand and after a second's hesitation, SITTING BULL takes it.*

SITTING BULL:
My people need ammunition.

WALSH: *beginning his "government" statement*
The Queen will not tolerate raiding from her soil, nor
does she. . . .

SITTING BULL:
Hard times have come to us. My warriors use the
lasso to bring down meat.

> *WALSH stares at him for a split second and decides to
> trust him.*

WALSH:
Ammunition will be issued sufficient for hunting
purposes. McCutcheon, take the Constable and see
to it.

McCUTCHEON:
Aye, sir!

> *McCUTCHEON and CLARENCE exit. The lights
> begin to dim.*

SITTING BULL:
We shall meet again.

WALSH: *smiling*
I look forward to it.

> *GALL, WALSH and SITTING BULL exit.*
> *PRETTY PLUME enters, unrolls a buffalo skin for the
> floor of the tent, as LOUIS, singing softly, removes his
> pack and sits a distance from the tent.*

LOUIS:
En roulant ma boule roulant, enroulant ma boule.
En roulant ma boule roulant, enroulant ma boule.
Derrier' chez nous, y' a-t'un e-tang, enroulant
ma boule,
Trois beaux canards s'en vont baignant, roulant
ma boule, roulant.

The lights brighten as McCUTCHEON and
CLARENCE enter, carrying bowls of food.
McCUTCHEON passes a bowl of food to LOUIS.

McCUTCHEON:
Here y'are, Louis.

McCUTCHEON and CLARENCE sit. All three
of them begin to eat. LOUIS eats with relish;
McCUTCHEON eats simply; CLARENCE sloshes his
bowl around, peering into it with apprehension. He is
reassured by LOUIS' appreciation of the contents. He
dips his fingers into the bowl and comes up with
something unpleasant. He quickly drops it back into the
bowl and grimaces. He looks at McCUTCHEON, who
tilts his bowl a bit and drains it. CLARENCE
swallows and looks down at his bowl. LOUIS glances
over at him.

LOUIS: *teasing CLARENCE*
Dat some good, eh?

CLARENCE smiles weakly and nods half-heartedly.
LOUIS gets up.

'Nother one?

He holds out his hand to take his bowl.

McCUTCHEON: *putting his empty bowl down*
Not for me, Louis.

LOUIS looks at CLARENCE.

CLARENCE:
I still got some. Thanks anyway.

LOUIS exits to get some more.

McCUTCHEON: *calling after him*
My compliments to the chef, Louis!

*CLARENCE stares at McCUTCHEON,
then down at his own bowl. McCUTCHEON
suppresses a smile.*

Laddie, ye better be eatin' that up, if ye want to keep
your forelock.

CLARENCE:
What do you mean?

McCUTCHEON: *whispering to him*
It's a great insult not to eat what's put before ye when
y're visitin' the Sioux. . . . Men have been known to
lose their scalps over such an insult.

CLARENCE: *sickly*
That so?

*He dips his fingers into his bowl again, comes in contact
with something unpleasant, drops it back into the bowl,
sits for a second, then makes up his mind.*

Well, I don't give a damn! I'd sooner be scalped than
eat any more of this stuff! Here, you take it!

McCUTCHEON laughs and pushes the bowl away.

McCUTCHEON:
I've done my duty, laddie. Now it's up to you.

LOUIS returns, dejected.

LOUIS:
　　Merde, McCutch. Dey eat it all up. Dere's none left.

　　CLARENCE looks up, brightens.

CLARENCE:
　　Say, Louis, I think...

　　He feels his forehead.

　　... I think I overdid it a bit today... don't really feel
　　too much like eatin' tonight.... If you want mine,
　　well, no sense seein' it wasted.

　　He offers his bowl hopefully to LOUIS.
　　LOUIS smiles, recognizing his ploy.

LOUIS:
　　Dat so? Weeeellllll....

　　He takes his bowl, squats and eats. CLARENCE
　　smiles at McCUTCHEON.

McCUTCHEON:
　　Now I wonder how the Major's makin' out.

LOUIS:　*looking up*
　　Da Major and Sittin' Bull over in da big tipi dere.
　　Dey send Louis away, but he keep an eye out all da
　　same.

　　He goes back to his food. McCUTCHEON gets
　　out his pipe and stretches his legs, but remains
　　sitting.

McCUTCHEON:
　　The Sioux have behaved themselves, there's no
　　denyin' that. Six months, it's been, and they're as
　　good as gold.

*LOUIS puts down his bowl and looks at
McCUTCHEON.*

LOUIS:

Dese Sioux, dey not stupid, you know. Make trouble
and dey know what happens. 'Mericans send Longknives up here. Dey kill every Indian dey see—little
ones, big ones, mama with bébé—dey don't give a
good goddamn, friendly or hostile. . . . You got red
skin . . .

He points his finger.

. . . bang-bang! . . . Louis' skin got reddish tinge.

*There is an awkward silence. The lights dim a bit.
McCUTCHEON and CLARENCE look down.
LOUIS shrugs and gets out his pipe.*

McCUTCHEON: *passing LOUIS his pouch of tobacco*
Try mine.

LOUIS takes the tobacco and fingers it.

LOUIS:
You buy new one, eh?

McCUTCHEON:
I got it at the post before we left. Feel that
leather . . . soft, isn't it?

LOUIS:
Dat's nice. . . .

He gazes off into space.

But not so nice as 'nother pouch I see once . . . many
year ago, before the redcoats come . . . I see white
man at Fort Whoop-Up, a Longknife. . . . He show
everybody mighty nice tobacco pouch he have . . .
made from breast of Indian woman he killed at Sand
Creek.

52

He looks in the direction of SITTING BULL's tipi.
McCUTCHEON and CLARENCE follow suit. As the
lights dim on them, they begin to come up on the tipi.
There is a soft background sound of Indian rattles and
bells, which continues in the background until the scene
with SITTING BULL is established. WALSH and
SITTING BULL are eating. WALSH looks up from
his bowl after a moment.

WALSH:
Louis tells me you've been visitin' the Blackfoot and
the Cree.

SITTING BULL:
They tell me that Major Walsh is the White
Forehead Chief . . . and the White Forehead Chief is
the Indian's friend. If trouble strikes your camp,
they say, send for the White Forehead Chief.

WALSH:
The Blackfoot. . . .

SITTING BULL:
Do you ride out to speak only of the Blackfoot and
the Cree. . . . Have you no news for the Sioux?

WALSH:
Yes, I have news . . . and it's not good news. . . . My
chief says the Queen is not responsible for you.

He holds up the George III medal.

This happened a long time ago. The Great White
Mother has made peace with the Americans.

SITTING BULL: *with a hint of sarcasm*
Whose red children are we then?

WALSH:
It was decided the Sioux belonged to the President in
Washington.

SITTING BULL:
It was decided. . . . You are few and we are many.
Will you try to drive us back across the line?

WALSH:
You're welcome to stay here so long as your young
men don't cross the line to raid and so long as the
Sioux are self-sufficient. . . . The Queen won't feed or
clothe you as she does her own Indians.

SITTING BULL: *leaning toward WALSH*
My people have never accepted the annuities. . . . We
have never touched the pen. . . . We have never sold
our land! It has been stolen from us! You need not
feed or clothe us. The Hunkpapa Lakota feed and
clothe themselves!

WALSH: *speaking gently*
Soon you won't be able to do that. The buffalo will
be gone. You must return to your home before that
happens.

SITTING BULL:
The Black Hills is our home! And the white man has
stolen them! I cannot sign away the Black Hills.
They are not mine alone. Before me, they were my
father's. After me, they shall be my children's. Do
you sign away the birthright of your children?

WALSH:
I tell you this because I am a soldier and I must
follow orders, but I am a friend also. White
Forehead . . .

He indicates himself.

. . . does not say this, Major Walsh says this.

He speaks officially.

The President in Washington has requested the Sioux
to return . . . and promises fair treatment to all.

*SITTING BULL stares at WALSH for a moment,
then begins to speak conversationally, casually.*

SITTING BULL:
Let me tell you what I have heard today. . . . Today, I
have news of my good friend Crazy Horse of the
Oglala. He was a dreamer, wishing only to serve his
people . . . and they loved him well. . . . Brave in
battle. Wise in council. He loved the little children
and could not bear to see them suffer. The Oglala
and the Hunkpapa fought together at the Greasy
Grass where Custer died. I brought my people across
the line, but Crazy Horse and the Oglala remained
behind. Since that time, they've known no peace.
General Terry pursued them like a wolf who tears at
the soft underbelly of a fleeing doe. . . . There are
two reservation chiefs across the line named Red
Cloud and Spotted Tail. Some say they are paper
chiefs created by the white man to betray their red
brothers. . . . Red Cloud and Spotted Tail met
Crazy Horse in council and begged him to bring his
people in, to touch the pen, to lead a reservation life.
They told him: "You will be a great chief!" . . . The
Sioux are proud; we love position. . . . My good friend
Crazy Horse is dead. He brought his people in and
when he stepped into the meeting place, he saw the
windows all were barred and 'round about stood
soldiers pointing longknives at him . . . and when he
turned to run, his arms were pinioned by his red
brothers and a white soldier pushed his bayonet into
Crazy Horse's stomach! It took one night for him to
die. He sang his death song and his mother and
father stood outside and sang back, for the white
soldiers would not let them enter where he lay dying.
And where he stood when he was struck, there is a
great gouge gone from the wall, for the soldier's
longknife passed through Crazy Horse and lodged
there till he withdrew it. . . . I am told that men with

skin like yours gaze at that gouge and laugh and joke and say: "There stood a good Indian . . . a dead Indian." . . . My good friend Crazy Horse of the Oglala.

WALSH:

Aren't things sometimes done in your name? Things you do not wish? It can be that way with white men too. , . . I am your friend.

SITTING BULL:

I have no white friends.

WALSH: .

For Christ's sake, forget the colour of our skin! If you've got no more to say than that, let's all line up and have it out! To hell with it! Is that what you want?

SITTING BULL:

Red men choke and die on white men's words!

WALSH:

When have my actions betrayed my words? I came here to speak to you as a man and I expect the same from you! What's past is past! Crazy Horse is dead, but others live and you and I are here to talk of them! . . . People are coming from the White Father in Washington. I ask you to see them. If you don't want to return with them, I will tell them so. I promise you, I'll stand by you.

SITTING BULL:

Who do they send?

WALSH:

General Terry.

SITTING BULL:
>You ask me to see this man? The man who burnt my mother earth and killed my friends! You tell me, see this man!

WALSH:
>If you wish to negotiate a reservation here in Canada, you must make your peace with the Americans first. *There is silence as WALSH and SITTING BULL sit staring at one another.*
>
>There's something more I have to say. . . . Last night, two men rode into your camp.

SITTING BULL:
>With news of Crazy Horse.

WALSH:
>And news of something more than that, I think.

SITTING BULL:
>They had a request to make of me.

WALSH:
>Nez Percés, weren't they?

SITTING BULL:
>Nez Percés . . . from the valley of the Winding Waters.

WALSH:
>The Wallowa Valley no longer belongs to them.

SITTING BULL:
>A thief treaty . . . Chief Joseph did not sign!

WALSH:
>Nevertheless, the President has put aside a reservation and the Indians must go onto it.

SITTING BULL:

What right has he to tell the Indian where he must go in his own land?

WALSH:

Is Chief Joseph trying to bring his people into Canada?

SITTING BULL:

I tell you what you already know . . . the Nez Percés are on the run. They have come to me. They request the Sioux to help them fight their way across the line.

WALSH:

What I do not know is your decision.

SITTING BULL:

I have not made it.

WALSH:

Then listen to me. If it can be proven that you've carried out an act of war against the Americans while camping here in Canada, your refuge will be in jeopardy.

SITTING BULL:

What could you do?

WALSH:

We could open the border and allow the American Army in to drive you out.

SITTING BULL:

Even though you know you send us to our death?

WALSH:

We don't know that.

SITTING BULL:

As we speak, Nez Percés are rotting, their bodies full of bullet holes, their heads smashed in with gunstocks and bootheels. Would you term this a natural death?

WALSH:

You see my red coat ... it represents the Queen and the Canadian government. My duty is to inform you of my government's position ... and it is this: "Armed excursions across the line ... for whatever reason ... will not be tolerated!"

He speaks gently to SITTING BULL.

I'd advise you to deny the Nez Percés.

SITTING BULL:

Men, women, children? ... They have travelled 1,300 miles.

WALSH:

Another 60 and they're across the line. My government won't try to stop them, but you must not try to aid them either. They must make it on their own.

SITTING BULL:

You ask me to deny them.

WALSH:

It's for the good of your people. You can see that.

SITTING BULL:

Yes ... I can see it. ... Today is a sad day for me. ... In the past, I have risen, tomahawk in hand. I have done all the hurt to the whites that I could. ... Now you are here. My arms hang to the ground as if dead. ... I believe the Blackfoot and the Cree have judged you wisely. I will call you White Sioux and I will trust you. I will speak to General Terry ... and I will deny the Nez Percés.

*As the lights dim on WALSH and SITTING BULL,
they come up blue and cold along with a background
sound of the howling wind. The lights pick out
McCUTCHEON and CLARENCE, who are
bundled in greatcoats. A winter blizzard is blowing.*

McCUTCHEON: *to CLARENCE who has stopped in front of
him* What is it?
CLARENCE:
We've lost the Major.

McCUTCHEON:
Keep goin', laddie.

CLARENCE:
We've lost the Major.

McCUTCHEON:
Here, let me. . . .

*He moves ahead of CLARENCE and begins walking,
holding his hand up to shield himself from the wind.
CLARENCE follows him.*

And we've no lost the Major. . . . Come on, laddie,
we'll wait for Louis here.

He and CLARENCE huddle together.

CLARENCE:
My God, I'm cold!

*A blue light picks out WALSH, SITTING BULL and
GALL as they enter in single file, leaning against the
storm.*

McCUTCHEON: *cupping his hand and calling*
Over here, sir!

WALSH: *as they approach*
Any sign of Louis?

McCUTCHEON shakes his head.

McCUTCHEON:
   Are ye sure Sittin' Bull's information is correct?

WALSH looks at SITTING BULL.

SITTING BULL:
   The Longknives have surrounded the Nez Percés, but
   some have broken through.

WALSH:
   Well, if they're out there, Louis'll find them.

CLARENCE:
   Aren't you worried 'bout him?

McCUTCHEON:
   Ah, we've got naught to worry about Louis. . . .
   He can look after himself.

CLARENCE:
   My God, I'm cold!

> *They hear a noise. They all turn around and look. A
> blue light picks out LOUIS. He makes his way toward
> them. He comes to SITTING BULL and stands before
> him without speaking. There is a pause for a moment.*

WALSH:
   Well . . . speak up, Louis, have the Nez Percés
   crossed the border?

LOUIS: *speaking to SITTING BULL*
   I have found da tracks of a small number of people.
   Dey have few ponies and move slowly. Most are on
   foot. . . . Dere trail is easy to follow . . . it is marked
   with frozen blood. . . . Come with me.

> *SITTING BULL and GALL prepare to follow him.
> He speaks to WALSH.*

61

LOUIS:
>Wait here. We speak to dem first. Dey will be
>frightened. We will bring dem back.

>>*They exit. There is silence. McCUTCHEON moves
>>toward WALSH, who stands at the edge of the light
>>looking out. A wolf howls. There is silence again, then
>>the whinnying of a pony. WALSH points.*

McCUTCHEON:
>Is it them, sir?

>>*SITTING BULL returns without his outer robes. He
>>wears leggings and breeches. He stands outside the circle
>>of light, a silhouette.*

WALSH:
>Sergeant... Constable.... Help them!

>>*He nods his head briskly in the direction from which
>>SITTING BULL came. He gives them his greatcoat.
>>They exit quickly.*

SITTING BULL: *an honest question*
>How does the white man sustain himself beneath the
>weight of the blood that he has shed?

>>*WALSH looks at SITTING BULL, then off at the
>>muffled sounds of people approaching. The light begins
>>to flicker, as if people were passing in front of it.
>>WALSH turns slowly, looking outside of the light. The
>>sound of people moaning is heard. A blue light picks out
>>CLARENCE as he makes his way toward WALSH.*

CLARENCE:
>Is... is it all right, sir? My coat... I've... I've given
>it to...

>>*He indicates vaguely outside of the light.*

... to ... to a little girl and her brother. Their feet
are frozen, sir.... Will the government mind about
the coat?

WALSH: *holding himself erect, military*
I'll speak on your behalf, Constable.

CLARENCE:
It's just women and children ... and a few men.
... Most of them are ... got wounds of one kind or
another. Chief Joseph, he's not with them.
He ... didn't make it.... It's only just people, people
that's been hurt! I don't see what they could have
done to deserve this.... Do you know what they've
done?

WALSH:
There ... see there....

*He hurriedly removes his tunic. He has on a long
underwear top.*

Take this ... take this to the woman on the
pony ... there ... with the papoose on her back.
Take it to her.

CLARENCE:
Yes, sir.

*He moves toward the figure and freezes a ways
from her. The wind howls. LOUIS stands on the
rim of the light, watching. CLARENCE returns,
moving slowly. He has the tunic with him.*

She doesn't need it ... she's been hit in the chest. The
baby's dead. It's got a bit of blood on it....

*He gives the tunic an ineffectual wipe, more a touch
of the blood, then looks at WALSH.*

CLARENCE:
>I didn't notice till I put it 'round her that . . . she didn't need it.

>>*WALSH slowly takes the tunic from him.*
>>*CLARENCE moves away as WALSH stands*
>>*there holding the tunic. He extends one arm slowly,*
>>*deliberately. He drops the tunic and looks out.*
>>*LOUIS steps forward, picks up the tunic and*
>>*hands it to WALSH.*

LOUIS:
>You can't just throw it away, sir. Dat's too easy.

>>*WALSH looks at him, takes the tunic and slowly*
>>*exits with it. LOUIS goes down on one knee.*
>>*SITTING BULL steps forward slightly. The*
>>*many voices of the Nez Percés are heard in the*
>>*background saying "Ay Ay" as LOUIS speaks.*

>My father has given me this nation.
>In protecting it,
>A hard time I have.

>Friends, hardships pursue me,
>Fearless of them,
>I live.
>My chiefs of old are gone.
>Myself, I shall take courage.

>>*The voices grow in volume. They stop simultaneously.*
>>*There is a second of blackout, then the light comes up on*
>>*PRETTY PLUME and CROWFOOT who are with*
>>*SITTING BULL, who is in his former position.*

PRETTY PLUME:
>Tatanka Yotanka!

>>*CROWFOOT runs toward SITTING BULL and*
>>*SITTING BULL picks him up, laughing. As he*
>>*swings him in the air, PRETTY PLUME approaches*

him and holds out a rawhide bag which contains sacred stones.

SITTING BULL:
Aha, Little One! Get to work, your mother says. Clear a spot.

CROWFOOT:
Now?

SITTING BULL:
Now.

> *He sits. CROWFOOT kneels, smoothing a spot to lay out the sacred stones, then he sits beside SITTING BULL. PRETTY PLUME sits watching from a distance.*

So. . . .

> *He arranges the stones in the shape of a Medicine Wheel.*

To the Great Spirit belongs all things. The four-legged and the two-legged . . . but to the two-legged he gives the power to make live and to destroy. . . . To you, he gives the cup of living water. . . . Now . . . see?

> *He indicates the circle of stones.*

It makes the sacred hoop. Here is the cross within the circle dividing it in four.

> *CLARENCE appears and stops before intruding. He draws near during the following speeches as he becomes interested.*

The Great Spirit caused everything to be in fours and four is a sacred number. Four directions — north, east, south, west; four divisions of time — the day, the night, the month, the year; four parts of everything that grows — the root, the stem, the leaves, the fruit. . . . What else?

CROWFOOT:
Ahhhhh. . . .

*SITTING BULL holds out his hands, palms down-
ward, his thumbs concealed. CROWFOOT thrusts out
his hands likewise.*

Four fingers on each hand . . . and . . . two arms, two
legs. . . .

He thrusts his limbs out, laughing.

Four in all!

CLARENCE casts a furtive look at his own hands.

SITTING BULL: *urging CROWFOOT on*
Four things above the earth — the sun . . . the moon. . . .

CROWFOOT:
The sky, the stars!

SITTING BULL smiles and nods at CROWFOOT.

SITTING BULL:
Good. . . . All of the universe is enclosed and revealed
in the sacred circle.

He traces the circle.   ✓

Do you see how the sundance is a sacred hoop . . .
and the sundance pole, the sacred centre? What
else?

CLARENCE: *caught up in it all, breaking in*
The tipi!

SITTING BULL looks at him.

Like, it's a circle too and . . . the fire . . . that's the
centre.

66

He shifts nervously, bumping one of the stones. He picks it up, then isn't sure where it goes. He hands it to SITTING BULL.

SITTING BULL: *holding up the stone*
This is a sacred stone. See how round it is. Everything the Great Spirit does is done in a circle. The sun and moon are round; they come and go forth in a circle. The white man says the earth is round . . . and so are all the stars. What else?

CROWFOOT:
Birds make their nests round!

WALSH enters quietly.

SITTING BULL:
The winds whirl; the seasons form a great circle . . . and when we, the Sioux, meet as a nation, we set our tipis so. . . .

He describes an arc with the hand holding the stone.

The nation's hoop!

He puts the stone back in position, then looks at WALSH.

WALSH:
It's time.

CLARENCE: *scrambling to his feet*
I'm sorry, sir.

To SITTING BULL.

The Major has asked me to inform you that they're ready. Everything's ready.

SITTING BULL inclines his head acknowledging CLARENCE.

A light comes up on GENERAL TERRY in uniform.

SITTING BULL places a hand on his son's shoulder. They make their way to the meeting place with GENERAL TERRY. GALL appears and joins them as well.

PRETTY PLUME goes to leave.

SITTING BULL:
> Come. . . . come.

PRETTY PLUME joins them.

Eventually, GALL, SITTING BULL, CROWFOOT and PRETTY PLUME will range themselves for the meeting.

WALSH, LOUIS, CLARENCE and McCUTCHEON attend the meeting as well, CLARENCE almost sneaking in to observe; LOUIS, McCUTCHEON and WALSH there in a more formal sense.

McCUTCHEON joins GENERAL TERRY. He appears to be acting as a temporary aide de camp for him.

CLARENCE: *to WALSH, as they make their way to the meeting place*   I got detained, sir. I got caught up.

WALSH places a hand on his shoulder and gives it a reassuring clasp.

When they enter, GENERAL TERRY ignores SITTING BULL's entrance. It is as if the Indians are not present.

WALSH:
> General Terry.

TERRY:
>Ah, Walsh. Wonderful man you got here. Been looking after me like I was one of his own.

WALSH:
>And so he does for me.

TERRY:
>Great country you have here.

>*WALSH nods.*

>I'm impressed. Empty as yet, but a course that'll change. My God, man, the wagon trains never cease across the line, and its settlers that'll open it up ... economic base, possibilities endless. You follow me?

>*WALSH nods.*

>Heavy responsibility on you and me, of course. And what's imperative ... safety, progress ... is the elimination of the savage.

WALSH:
>Sir?

TERRY:
>Control of the savage, elimination of the savage aspects of the Indun's character. . . . Do you follow me? Though what you'd have left, be goddamned if I know.

>*He chuckles.*

>However, governments decree and we, poor bastards that we are, must deliver. . . .

>*He looks towards the Sioux and sighs, then looks back at WALSH.*

>You ever meet George?

WALSH:
General Custer?

TERRY:
Great tragedy that . . . and there are the very devils themselves. Savage, they may be, but I'll tell you this, Major, they are are kittens compared to the Eastern press. I'll take a Sioux sittin' on my chest anyday to a scribe peerin' over my shoulder. You follow me? You know where you are with a Sioux. Headlines coast to coast lauding George . . . and between you and me, he was a man had his faults. . . . Same goddamn papers up for court-martialing him over that Wichitas business, and now, up on a pedestal, and bring the villains to justice, wipe them out . . . and of course the government's got to act. . . . Do you follow me? And it's yours and my head on the block. . . . That's the way of it. That's what we live with. So . . . .

He look at the Sioux and sniffs. He whispers to WALSH confidentially.

And I'll tell you this . . . whatever we do, by the time we're finished, they'll have flip-flopped to the other side of the fence. You follow me?

WALSH does not follow him.

The papers, man, the Eastern press.

WALSH:
Yes, sir.

TERRY:
Not a man among them I'd have at my back in a fight.

He whispers.

Nor a position I'd give to George, if the truth be
known.

He chuckles, stops, clears his throat.

Still, a wonderful soldier, one of the best.

*He gets out a pair of wire-rimmed glasses, studies a
document and looks up.*

I am empowered to speak to you on behalf of the
American government.

PRETTY PLUME:
We are listening.

GENERAL TERRY looks at her, then continues.

TERRY:
The Great White Father in Washington is a generous
father.

PRETTY PLUME:
We are listening.

TERRY:
Who the hell is she? . . . Your deeds against the whites
have been grievous. The mighty arm and righteous
anger of the Great White Father has been raised
against you. It is within his power to wipe you out.
He has stayed that anger and that might. He has
forgiven you.

PRETTY PLUME:
We are listening.

TERRY:
They got a goddamn woman speaking for them. . . .
Who speaks for the Sioux?

SITTING BULL:

> The bearer of our children.

TERRY:

> I'm here to speak to you!

PRETTY PLUME:

> We are listening.

TERRY:

> The Great White Father holds your lives in his hand. The Indian is his . . . to do with as he pleases. You will return across the line. A reservation has been provided for you and you will go on it. Goods will be provided sufficient for your needs. Should you heed my words, you will be safe in the hand of the Great White Father. Should you not. . . .

> > *He closes his hand tightly and makes a gesture of throwing away.*

PRETTY PLUME:

> We have heard you.

TERRY:

> Get her out of here.

> > *McCUTCHEON looks at WALSH.*

> Get her out! I'm here to talk to you!

> > *The Sioux start to leave.*

> Who the hell do they think they are? Stop them!

> > *The Sioux exit, except for SITTING BULL.*

WALSH:

> Do you realized what he's promised? A reservation, food and supplies for your people, an amnesty. No one will be punished or go to jail for acts of war

72

committed against the government. All that will be
forgiven and forgotten!

SITTING BULL:

Forgotten? . . . When I was a boy, the Sioux owned
the world. The sun rose and set on our land. We sent
10,000 men to battle. Where are those warriors
now? Who slew them? Where are our lands? Who
owns them? Tell me . . . what law have I broken? Is it
wrong for me to love my own? Is it wicked for me
because my skin is red? Because I am Sioux, because
I was born where my fathers lived, because I would
die for my people and my country? . . . This white
man would forgive me . . . and while he speaks to me
of forgiveness, what do his people say in secret?
"Seize their guns and horses! Drive them back across
the line! The more we kill this year, the less we have
to kill next year." Is it not true?

TERRY:

Goddamn waste of time.

> *He thrusts his fist towards SITTING BULL, then
> makes a throwing away gesture, and leaves.
> McCUTCHEON follows. LOUIS remains as
> SITTING BULL and WALSH speak. There is a
> pause. Eventually, SITTING BULL turns to
> WALSH and begins intimately.*

SITTING BULL:

You are a white man. The God whose son you killed
must love you and your people well, for he has
rewarded you with many gifts . . . and tools . . .
and . . .

> *He indicates their uniforms, their guns, etc.*

. . . all this. . . . I am told wisdom is yours as well.
Advise me now, White Sioux. Tell me what is best
for my people. I will follow your advice . . . and the
burden of it will be on your shoulders. . . .

WALSH does not answer him.

SITTING BULL:

Shall I lead my people into the arms of the
Longknives? Will they protect us as "feathers do a
bird"? . . . Look inside your heart! . . . You have a
heart. I saw it the night the Nez Percés crossed the
line. What does your heart say?

WALSH: *agitated*

You know, if you refuse this offer, there'll be nothing
for you here. My government says they won't feed
you or give you reservations.

SITTING BULL:

Is your advice then to return with the Americans?

WALSH:

My advice . . . is . . . to consider . . . to consider the
consequences of your actions. That is my advice.

SITTING BULL:

What does that mean?

WALSH:

It means . . . if you stay . . . you're dependent on
the buffalo . . . and when they go, as they are surely
going, we won't care for you as we do our own
Indians. . . . Now, if you go with General Terry, he
has given his word that you won't be mistreated
or. . . .

He stops himself from saying the word "killed."

You will be fed and clothed.

SITTING BULL:

Would you choose to live as you advise me to do?

WALSH:

I don't advise you to do this. I . . . merely state your
choices.

SITTING BULL:
>   I know many who took the white man's promise...
>   Bear Ribs, White Antelope, Iron Shield, Black
>   Kettle, Stirring Bear... Crazy Horse. I would ask
>   their guidance, but all of them are dead.

WALSH:
>   You... make your point.

SITTING BULL: *dropping all pretense of asking for advice*
>   Let us speak clearly to each other... if.the President
>   in Washington can say: "Come, you are safe here"
>   and then change his mind and let the Longknives kill
>   us.... Can it not work the other way too?

>   *He looks intently at WALSH.*

>   Cannot the Great White Mother say: "No food or
>   reservations," but then reconsider? Our brothers, the
>   Santee Sioux, from across the line...

WALSH:
>   ... have been given a reservation in Manitoba. Quite
>   right!

SITTING BULL: *opening up to WALSH, stating his secret fear*
>   I believe the Americans are only waiting to get us all
>   together... and then they will slaughter us. That is
>   what I believe.

>   *WALSH thinks, then decides.*

WALSH:
>   Right!... Well now, I've delivered my government's
>   message, to which your reply is....

SITTING BULL:
>   The Sioux are self-sufficient!

WALSH:
>   Mmmm... and I shall give your final decision to
>   General Terry, that is....

SITTING BULL: *joking*
Tell him he can take it easy on the way back. The
Sioux only fight with men.

WALSH: *smiling*
I was thinking of something a bit more formal.

SITTING BULL: *begins by playing the role a bit*
He came here to tell us lies, but we don't want to
hear them. . . . I intend to stay here . . . and to raise
my people in this country.

> *SITTING BULL leaves. The lights begin to fade.*
> *WALSH looks after him for a moment, then begins to*
> *leave.*

LOUIS: *speaking from the shadows*
Major!

> *WALSH stops and looks at LOUIS.*

Does da Major know what month dis is?

WALSH:
The month when the green grass comes up.

LOUIS: *without humour*
Major damn good pupil.

WALSH: *almost abruptly*
Louis damn good teacher.

> *He turns to go.*

LOUIS: *moving toward WALSH*
Louis "request" permission to speak to da Major.

WALSH: *with a trace of irritation*
Here and now?

LOUIS:

Last fall, crossin' da Milk River, da Major's horse
step in dat sink hole . . . and Louis, he grab da Major
and pull 'im out. . . .

WALSH nods.

Da other year, when Louis hear all kind of story
'bout da 'ssiniboine makin' trouble . . . Louis tell da
Major . . . even t'ough dat 'ssiniboine is son of good
friend of Louis' mother. . . .

WALSH:

The Major is in your debt.

LOUIS:

And some of Louis' mother's people don't speak to
him no more, but dis don't matter, for Louis trust da
Major to do da right thing. . . . Dis is da month when
da green grass come up, da moon of makin' fat; dis is
spring. . . . Can da Major make da spring come for da
Sioux? What can you do for Sittin' Bull?

WALSH:

Everything within my power.

LOUIS:

How much is dat?

WALSH:

Say what you mean, Louis

LOUIS:

Louis choose to trust, but da Indian can do nothin'
else but trust. . . . Trust . . . or die. . . . Sometime, trust
and die. . . . Can da Major make da spring come for
da Sioux?

WALSH:

You trust in me . . . and I trust in those above
me. . . . Quite simple, eh? . . . Now, let's get on. . . .

He goes to leave.

LOUIS:
> Da Indian say he would trust da Great White Mother more if she did not have so many bald-headed thieves workin' for her!

WALSH stops and turns.

WALSH: *angrily*
> The Sioux have a case . . . a strong case . . . and I shall present it!

LOUIS: *softly*
> Who stands behind you dere?

WALSH:
> Honourable men!

LOUIS spits.

Blackout.

Act Two

The lights come up on HARRY, CLARENCE,
LOUIS and McCUTCHEON. The lights are
punctuated by LOUIS throwing his knife into the floor of
the stage. A dull thud is heard. LOUIS sits with his
rifle unslung; McCUTCHEON sits cleaning his saddle.
CLARENCE is attempting to thread a needle. As
HARRY watches the three of them, McCUTCHEON
leans over, picks up the needle from CLARENCE,
threads it efficiently and passes it back. CLARENCE
looks up at McCUTCHEON.

CLARENCE:
Thanks. . . .

He begins to mend a sock. HARRY and
McCUTCHEON exchange a look of amusement.

HARRY:
Sewin' detail, eh?

He begins to roll a cigarette as he watches CLARENCE.

CLARENCE: *intent on his sewing*
Yeah . . . I wish me Mum were here. . . .

*McCUTCHEON tosses HARRY a match for his
cigarette.*

CLARENCE:
> This ain't my idea of police work.

McCUTCHEON:
> Ah, laddie, your poor wee face would have been wet
> with tears for your Mum if ye'd been with the force
> on our march west in '73. I don't know what ye'd
> have called that.

HARRY: *settling down to watch everyone work*
> It weren't the Mounted Police then, Clarence, it were
> the Dismounted Police.... Lost practically every
> horse they had.

> *He laughs.*

McCUTCHEON:
> Aye, a man with the best will in the world couldn't
> call it the force's finest hour.

LOUIS:
> Dey didn't have Louis with dem. Dey need a good
> scout.

McCUTCHEON:
> I never saw so many bugs... blackflies so thick they
> clogged your nose so ye couldn't draw breath... and
> every man from the Colonel down infected with fleas.
> It's a lovely time y're havin', laddie. Ye don't
> appreciate it.

CLARENCE:
> Yeah... well... me Mum always mended my things
> at home.

HARRY:
> Jesus Christ, Clarence, you had a good thing there,
> boy, your Mum waitin' on you hand an' foot. What'd

you want to go and join up for? You could have had
it easy in the East.

CLARENCE:
My dad was a soldier.

HARRY:
You don't say?

CLARENCE:
Yup. Half-pay officer, served in the Crimean, he
did.... And, after that, he and me Mum, they come
out to Upper Canada in '60. First winter out, my
Dad, he died.... I can't hardly remember him.
... But, me Mum, she used to tell me 'bout him bein'
a soldier and all.... It was hard goin' for us.... I
think me Mum was the real soldier....

McCUTCHEON:
No brothers or sisters, laddie?

CLARENCE:
Nope.... Mum's all alone back East.

HARRY:
You ain't told us why you joined?

CLARENCE:
Well... me Mum, she said I was a man like my
Dad... and I had to find my own place... couldn't
sit in Glengarry growin' potatoes and tendin' to her.
And she was right.... I got to thinking....

HARRY:
Yeah?

CLARENCE:
You all'd laugh.

HARRY:
No, we wouldn't.

CLARENCE:

romantic dude

Well, I got to thinkin', out here in the territories, that was where everything was happenin'... the Indian Wars... and openin' the West... and Wild Bill Hickock sittin' on the biggest, blackest horse you ever saw!

He looks at HARRY, McCUTCHEON and LOUIS, who regard him seriously.

I wanted to do what was right... and excitin' and... and make me Mum proud of me.

McCUTCHEON looks out at the horizon and sniffs.

HARRY:

How do you figure it's turned out?

CLARENCE:

I guess she's proud of me.... Not so excitin' as I thought it'd be... and as far as what's right goes... that don't seem to come into it....

McCUTCHEON:

What's that in the air, Louis? Smoke?

LOUIS:

Lotta smoke.... Dere goin' be more.

CLARENCE:

I don't smell nothin!.

HARRY:

Hell, Clarence, you won't smell it till tomorrow or next day.... The Sergeant here, he smells it today... and Louis.

He smiles at LOUIS.

When'd you smell it, Louis?

LOUIS: *holding up two fingers*
Two days ago.

CLARENCE:
What's it from?

LOUIS:
Da 'mericans fire da border.

CLARENCE: *curious*
What?

LOUIS:
'Merican soldiers, da Longknives, dey set fires all
'long da border, two or three hundred mile long,
every ten mile or so.

CLARENCE: *to McCUTCHEON*
What's he sayin'? That don't make sense, Louis.

LOUIS:
Make a lotta sense.

HARRY:
It's this way, Clarence.... The buffalo across the line
start movin' north, so the soldiers burn all along the
border. The buffalo turn back and then the American
government don't have to feed the reservation
Indians.

CLARENCE looks at him blankly.

They're suppose to hunt and feed themselves!

CLARENCE:
Well, what about *our* Indians?

LOUIS: *surprised*
You got some Indians?

CLARENCE:
You know what I mean.

LOUIS ignores him and looks at his gun.

Okay. . . . What about *the* Indians livin' on the Canadian side of the line?

LOUIS:
What about dem?

CLARENCE:
What're they suppose to do?

HARRY:
Eat grass.

CLARENCE: *angrily*
I don't believe you! Besides, I don't smell nothin'. It's all a lie. There's no smoke in the air! Do you smell smoke, Sergeant?

McCUTCHEON:
Look at that haze over the hills, laddie.

CLARENCE:
That's a heat haze . . . from the sun.

HARRY:
You think so, eh?

CLARENCE:
Well, I don't believe it! It ain't fair! And even if it was true . . . and there weren't no buffalo . . . and nothin' for them to eat, well then, the Canadian government, it'd send out food for them. It's got a responsibility!

LOUIS: *shrugging*
Maybe so.

HARRY:
So the Canadian government feeds its own
Indians.... Who's gonna feed the Sioux?

CLARENCE:
They're people, aren't they?

McCUTCHEON, HARRY and LOUIS look at him.

You don't let people starve to death, do you? Just
'cause you wish they'd move someplace else, you don't
let people starve! You can't do things like that. You
can't do things like that!

*He stares at HARRY, McCUTCHEON and LOUIS.
They all freeze. HARRY pulls a document out and reads
from it. The lights slowly dim.*

HARRY:
MacDonald reports that though the Sioux have
behaved themselves remarkably well since crossing
into Canada, their presence in the North West
Territories has been attended by serious
consequences. The buffalo are rapidly diminishing
and the advent of so large a body of foreign Indians
has precipitated their diminution. The Sioux are
already feeling the hardship and are hard pressed to
avert danger and suffering from famine.

*The lights black out. About four bars of calliope music is
heard. The lights come back up. MARY is sitting there
embroidering. WALSH is a distance away from her. The
music fades as WALSH speaks.*

WALSH:
My... dearest... Mary.... My dearest Mary.

MARY:
Jim.

85

WALSH:

Two letters came in today . . . along with a load of winter supplies. I don't know which I was happier to see.

MARY:

The girls are fine. . . . It's been a long time since they've seen you.

WALSH:

You'll think I've got a touch of prairie fever, but the solitude here, the emptiness of these Great Plains, fills me with a sense of timelessness.

MARY:

Both send their love.

WALSH:

Remember the day we picnicked on the river? Cora, plump and placid on the blanket; little Mary showing me her hands stained with the juice of flowers . . . and you bent over the basket, your hair hanging loose and laughing. . . . You looked eighteen.

MARY:

I hope you're looking after yourself.

She laughs.

How often do I say that?

WALSH:

You're not to worry about my health. McCutcheon's like a mother hen.

MARY:

Here in the East, we're always hearing grand tales of Major Walsh . . . how he's subdued the Sioux and Sitting Bull.

WALSH:

The Sioux.... Common sense, honesty and
humanity.

MARY:

The treachery.

WALSH:

Ah, Mary, we call our actions strategy or tactics;
we call theirs treachery.... My God, if I could only
show you what I see every day.... The buffalo are
gone, vanished... like frost at dawn... one minute
here, the next... nowhere. In the fall, the Sioux were
hungry. Now, it's winter... and they starve.

MARY:

After church supper, the choir sang.

WALSH:

Sickness, plain suffering kills them like flies. Most of
their ponies are dead... and their rotting carcasses
are cut up for food.... Yes, they're starving and
destitute, yet they endure. They share what little they
have... and they observe the law. Goddamnit, they'd
be a credit to any community.... Ottawa has not
acknowledged my recommendations....

MARY: *smiling*
You always say don't worry.

WALSH:

I wonder if Dewdney has even forwarded them.

MARY:

But, of course, I worry. It's natural to worry.

She laughs.

Yesterday I found another grey hair. You won't know
me when you return.

WALSH:

    I try to understand the government's viewpoint. . . .
Jesus Christ, I'm no raw recruit! One thing I know,
across the line there's been gross and continual
mismanagement of the Sioux. An able and brilliant
people have been crushed, held down, moved from
place to place, cheated and lied to. . . . And now, they
hold on here in Canada, the remnants of a proud
race, and they ask for some sort of justice . . . which is
what I thought I swore an oath to serve!

    The lights begin to fade.

MARY: *distant*

    Your "little" Mary's soon to be thirteen. . . . Don't
forget her birthday, will you?

WALSH:

    We carried great bouquets of flowers home that
day. . . .

    He looks down at his hands.

She's not thirteen. . . .

MARY:

    Cora's getting thin.

WALSH:

    Cora, red and bawling; and you with your hair
spread on the pillow, smiling and offering me your
hand. . . .

    *The lights go out on MARY. There is a spotlight on the
figure of WALSH.*

The girls, still babies; you, eighteen, in the East
. . . suspended in amber . . . while I grow old in the
West. . . .

McCUTCHEON:
> Colonel MacLeod to see you, sir.

WALSH:
> MacLeod? Send him on in.

> *MacLEOD enters. WALSH springs up to greet him
> sincerely. Both are original members of the force and are
> friends.*

> Welcome to the fort, Colonel. Pleasant journey,
> I trust?

MacLEOD:
> Not bad, Major, not bad. . . . You're looking well.

McCUTCHEON:
> Is there anything else, sir?

WALSH:
> No, McCutcheon. Stand down.

> *McCUTCHEON leaves.*

MacLEOD:
> To tell the truth, Jim, you look like death. What the
> hell have you been up to?

WALSH:
> If you think I look bad, you should see the horses.

MacLEOD:
> That so?

WALSH:
> It's been a hard winter.

MacLEOD: *clipping the end of a cigar*
> Seems to be the case right across the West.

WALSH gets out a flask and looks at MacLEOD who nods "yes" to a drink.

WALSH:
> Are you doing the tour early? The boys at Fort Walsh are always on their toes. It'll be a . . . .

MacLEOD:
> Nothing like that.

WALSH: *stiffening somewhat*
> Do you bring news for the Sioux?

MacLEOD:
> Sit down, Jim. I'd like a wee informal talk with you.

WALSH:
> Well now, you've caught my interest.

> *He sits down.*

> What is it?

> *There is a pause as MacLEOD examines the end of his cigar. He looks up at WALSH and pauses again.*

MacLEOD:
> Soooo . . . horses had a bad winter, eh?

WALSH:
> What the hell are you here for?

MacLEOD: *putting a letter on the desk*
> Recognize that?

WALSH: *looking at the letter and dropping it back on the desk*
> I usually recognize my own correspondence. It's a letter I sent Frank Mills at Fort Benton across the line. Why're you dropping it on my desk like a hot potato?

MacLEOD:

I'd be most surprised to hear that you're unaware of the proper channels one must go through when making a suggestion of the nature contained in this letter.

WALSH:

My note to Frank Mills suggests an exchange of stolen horses. American horses stolen by Canadian Indians to be exchanged for Canadian horses stolen by American Indians. . . . Hardly an international incident.

MacLEOD:

And what is the proper channel through which we should negotiate an arrangement like this?

WALSH:

The proper channel? Yes, sir. I should send a recommendation to my commanding officer, Colonel MacLeod. If he decides to act on it, he will send a recommendation to Ottawa. If it ever reaches the Prime Minister's office and he decides to act on it, he will send a recommendation to London. It is possible that London will send it to Washington, and Washington to Mills' commanding officer, and, God willing and the mails providing, Mills will receive a recommendation concerning the exchange of stolen horses. Jesus Christ, man! That's 6,000 miles and the Lord knows how many bureaucratic bunglers. Frank Mills is 60 miles south of me. Are you trying to tell me that you object to my simplifying matters?

MacLEOD:

It's not my objecting to it. . . . Mills, apparently, objects to it.

WALSH:

What the hell do you mean by that?

MacLEOD:

> He forwarded your "note" to Fort Robson. To make a long story short, the President has sent a formal protest to the Queen regarding the high-handed methods of a certain officer of the force serving the Canadian West. . . .

WALSH:

> Son-of-a-bitch!

> *To himself.*

> The next goddamn American horse the boys bring in, I'll have it shot.

MacLEOD:

> You realize as well as I do that this is only the tip of the iceberg.

WALSH: *back to MacLEOD*

> Where are you now, Colonel . . . back on the cold winter again?

MacLEOD:

> I'm talking abut the real reason for the American protest against your behaviour. I'm talking about Sitting Bull and the Sioux.

> *WALSH stiffens and becomes more formal.*

WALSH:

> I'm afraid I don't follow you, sir.

MacLEOD:

> Jim, the Americans believe . . . and they have convinced the Prime Minister . . . that you are privately urging Sitting Bull to remain in Canada while publicly stating that he must leave.

WALSH:
Which indicates how little they know of Sitting Bull. When his mind's made up, no man can sway him.

MacLEOD:
Not even his friends?

WALSH:
He has no white friends.

MacLEOD:
He calls you White Sioux. What is that suppose to mean?

WALSH:
We have an understanding.

MacLEOD:
Oh? . . . Which means?

WALSH:
We understand each other.

MacLEOD: *tapping the letter on the desk*
The protest over this is an attempt to discredit you and it all leads back to the Sioux. You're close to that old war horse. Persuade him to return across the line. Goddamn it, he's a thorn in our flesh. We can't discuss a bloody thing with the Americans without they bring it up!

WALSH:
What up?

MacLEOD:
Our giving sanctuary to those responsible for the Custer Massacre. They talk of nothing else.

WALSH:
Custer was responsible for the death of himself and his men! For Christ's sake, speak the truth!

93

MacLEOD:

I'm not here to argue with you. I'm here as a friend.

WALSH:

I've had my orders and I've followed them.

MacLEOD:

I'm asking you to do more than that. . . . He trusts you.

WALSH:

Because he knows I won't deceive him.

MacLEOD:

He'll listen to you.

WALSH:

Because he trusts me and he knows I won't deceive him.

MacLEOD: *softly*

How am I asking you to deceive him?

There is a pause.

The Sioux have no future here in Canada.

WALSH:

Tell me something. . . . It was you, as Commissioner of the North West Mounted Police, who impressed upon me that a part of my duty, no less important than the policing of this area, was the accurate observation and recording of events, no matter how minute. . . . Such a report, to be sent monthly, along with my recommendations for government policy.

MacLEOD:

Quite correct.

WALSH:

Then, why the hell is nothing acted upon?

MacLEOD:
>   Did you not receive two stallions, come in with
>   Harry, to sire your mares? Are you not now in the
>   act of digging a new well?

WALSH:
>   I'm not talking about domestic trivia! I don't need a
>   statement from the goddamn Prime Minister to
>   undertake a new well!

MacLEOD:
>   Ah, but you do, Jim.

WALSH:
>   My men are not in the act of digging a new well.
>   ... My men *dug* a new well two months before
>   permission was granted! The entire fort would have
>   been down with typhoid or dead of thirst had I
>   waited for word from Ottawa.

>   *MacLEOD sighs and shakes his head.*

>   What about my recommendations concerning the
>   Indians?

MacLEOD:
>   What about them?

WALSH:
>   The Sioux have as much legal right to a reservation
>   here as the Santee Sioux had in Manitoba.

MacLEOD:
>   The Santee Sioux did not kill Custer.

WALSH:
>   They killed over 600 white settlers in Minnesota who
>   were not engaged in an act of war against them. Why
>   are my recommendations not acted upon?

MacLEOD:

> Out here, you don't see the whole picture. There're
> other considerations.

WALSH:

> My recommendations are ignored! I may as well post
> them in the privy!

MacLEOD:

> You play chess. . . . Sometimes a pawn is sacrificed on
> one side of the board to gain an advantage on the
> other.

WALSH: *in disbelief*
> I am a pawn?

MacLEOD:

> No, no, Jim . . . not you. . . . It might be possible to
> consider Sitting Bull and the Sioux as pawns.

WALSH:

> What are the advantages to be gained from
> this . . . this sacrifice?

MacLEOD:

> We can't know that, can we? That's the kind of
> weighty decision the Prime Minister and London
> must contend with.

WALSH:

> I demand to know what advantage is to be gained.

MacLEOD:

> The Prime Minister is not responsible to you, Jim!

WALSH:

> Goddamn it, he is! If I carry out his orders, he is
> responsible to me.

MacLEOD:
You're talking nonsense. An army that operated like that couldn't navigate its way across a playing field! And you know it!

WALSH:
What do you think happens when I take off this tunic? At night, in my quarters, what do you think happens to me?

MacLEOD:
Jim. . . .

WALSH:
Do you think McCutcheon hangs me up from some goddamn wooden peg with all my strings dangling? Is that what you think happens? Do you think I'm a puppet? Manipulate me right and anything is possible. . . . I'm a person. I exist. I think and feel! And I will not allow you to do this to me!

MacLEOD: *softly*
To do what to you? I merely ask you to use your position with Sitting Bull to convince him to leave the country in the best interests of his people.

WALSH:
I've had my orders and I've followed them. . . .

MacLEOD:
You're tired, Jim.

WALSH:
Ask my men if I'm tired. No one at this post rises earlier or is to bed later. Fatigue is unknown to me.

MacLEOD:
You work yourself too hard.

WALSH:
I have a job and I do it.

MacLEOD:
It's a long time since you've been home.

WALSH:
Home? I don't request a leave of absence,
Colonel. . . . Shall we get on with the business at
hand?

MacLEOD:
I have two dispatches from the Prime Minister. The
first concerns the Sioux.

WALSH:
What is it?

MacLEOD:
You are to see that no food stuffs, clothing,
ammunition or supplies are given them . . . if they
do not possess the money to pay for them.

WALSH:
They have no money.

MacLEOD:
It has been brought to the attention of the Prime
Minister that certain settlers as well as members of
the force itself have been supplying the Sioux with
various odds and ends of food and clothing. This
must stop at once.

WALSH:
Yes, sir.

MacLEOD:
The Prime Minister feels that, whereas common
sense has not prevailed upon the Sioux, hunger will.

*He looks at WALSH for a moment, then back at his
dispatch.*

98

My second dispatch concerns your ill-advised note to
Major Mills.

WALSH:

Yes, sir.

MacLEOD:

An apology is to be written, couched in the
appropriate words, stating that you humbly beg the
American government's pardon for overstepping the
limits of your authority.

He pauses.

Is that understood?

WALSH:

I. . . .

MacLEOD:

If you find yourself unable to do this, it is my sad
duty to ask you for your resignation.

WALSH:

How well you know your men.

MacLEOD:

I pride myself on that.

WALSH:

They say one's strongest instinct is self-
preservation . . . and I've made the force my
life. . . . To whom do I send this letter?

MacLEOD:

To your commanding officer, myself, naturally.

WALSH:

Ah, yes.

MacLEOD:
> I'll see that it's forwarded to Ottawa. . . . Well, Jim,
> how about a walk around the post before bed? . . .
> Bit of pleasure after a surfeit of business.

WALSH:
> McCutcheon! . . . Sorry, Colonel, I've a few things to
> attend to. McCutcheon will see you to your quarters.
>
> *McCUTCHEON enters.*
>
> Goodnight, sir.

MacLEOD:
> Goodnight, Jim.
>
> *WALSH stands rigid until McCUTCHEON and
> McLEOD exit. When they have gone, he pours himself
> another drink. He walks outside of his office and stands
> looking at the prairies, flask in hand. We hear someone
> whistling "Garryowen." He listens to the whistling, then
> speaks.*

WALSH:
> That you, Harry?

HARRY:
> You give me a start there, Major. I didn't expect to
> see nobody up at this time of night.
>
> *WALSH takes a drink and extends the flask to
> HARRY.*
>
> Don't mind if I do.
>
> *He takes a drink and keeps the flask.*
>
> I been up visitin' with Sittin' Bull. . . . Always a dry
> night when you visit with the old man. . . . Lots of
> tobacco, but no booze.

WALSH:
> Fraternizing, eh?

HARRY:
> Oh, no, nothin' like that.... Just chewin' the fat.

There is a pause.

> Hear MacLeod come in today.... Bit early, ain't he?

There is another pause.

> Is he here for the tour?

WALSH: *bringing his attention back to HARRY*
> No, no... he isn't.

HARRY:
> O-fficial business, eh? O-fficial business.

WALSH:
> Do you know Brockville, Harry?

HARRY:
> Can't say as I do.

WALSH:
> Pretty town.... Trees. Shade in the summertime
> ... cool and green.

HARRY:
> Hell of a change from this place, I reckon.

WALSH:
> My wife lives in Brockville... and my two girls.

HARRY:
> Ain't got a son?

WALSH:
> No.... No son... just as well... no son. Pretty
> place, though.

HARRY:
> What the hell! Have another drink, Major!

> *He passes the flask to him.*

WALSH: *taking a drink and passing the flask back to HARRY*
> I've always been a man of principles, Harry. I've
> always thought of myself as a man of principle.
> ... Honour, truth, the lot. ... They're just words,
> Harry. They don't exist. I gave my life to them and
> they don't exist.

> *HARRY stares at WALSH.*

HARRY: *'uneasy*
> You should get to bed, Major. It ain't night, it's
> mornin'.

> *WALSH smiles.*

WALSH:
> Fatigue is unknown to me.

> *HARRY smiles back, feeling he's back on more familiar
> ground.*

HARRY:
> That's a fact, sir. That's a fact. Ain't never knowed
> you to be tired.

> *WALSH reaches for the flask, takes a drink and hands it
> back to HARRY.*

WALSH:
> You were up visiting the Sioux, were you?

HARRY:
> Yessireee. Course, they knowed MacLeod's come in.
> Naturally, they's wonderin' if it means anythin' for
> them.

WALSH:

Oh yes, I should say it does.

HARRY:

Good news?

WALSH:

The Sioux have no future here in Canada.

HARRY:

They sure as hell don't have none south of the line.

WALSH:

The government's concern stops at the border.

HARRY:

Major, you get yourself too het up.

WALSH:

I see . . . larger issues at stake.

HARRY:

Don't see what's a larger issue than a man's life. . . .
No Injun agent's gonna put up with Sittin' Bull.

WALSH:

You think not?

HARRY:

They'll kill him off. . . . Only smart thing to do, ain't
it?

WALSH:

And how do you feel about that?

HARRY:

Ain't nothin' I can do. . . . Goodnight, Major.

> *WALSH stares at HARRY as he exits, then he exits.*
> *PRETTY PLUME enters, carrying a pipe. She is*
> *followed by CROWFOOT.*

PRETTY PLUME: *singing*
Little One, Little One,
Loved by everyone.
Little One speaks sweet words to everyone.
That is why, that is why,
Little One is loved by everyone.

CROWFOOT puts his head in her lap in the semi-darkness outside of the scene. CLARENCE sneaks furtively into the light, carrying a small knapsack.

CLARENCE: *whispering*
Pssssstttt! . . . Little One! . . . Little One!

SITTING BULL: *from the shadows*
Is it my son you seek?

CLARENCE is frightened.

CLARENCE:
Oh! . . . Ah . . . yes, sir. I was just . . . a . . .

He tries to conceal the knapsack behind him.

. . . I was just . . . lookin' for your little boy.

SITTING BULL comes into the light. He looks older; his face is drawn.

SITTING BULL:
You are the young man who rides out with White Sioux . . . . Is he with you?

CLARENCE:
Ah, well, no sir. . . . I . . . come by myself. . . . I brought. . . .

He quickly thrusts the knapsack at SITTING BULL.

Ah . . .

He nods at the knapsack.

. . . some things from the mess, sir. I'd like the little boy to have them.

SITTING BULL takes the knapsack and nods his thanks.

SITTING BULL:
You have a good heart. . . . I have little to offer you in return. . . .

He sees the pipe that PRETTY PLUME has brought on. He checks his tobacco pouch and smiles.

Come! Have a pipe with me!

He sits and motions CLARENCE to sit.

CLARENCE:
Well, I . . . don't know if I should.

SITTING BULL:
Sit!

CLARENCE sits in silence as SITTING BULL prepares the pipe and passes it to him. There is silence as they smoke for a bit.

Times are bad. . . . They say there are still buffalo south of the line, but if we go to hunt them, the bluecoats will kill us.

He laughs dryly.

It hardly matters, as our ponies are too weak to carry us there in the first place. But my heart grows weak and trembles when I hear the little children cry for food. . . . It is a hard thing.

He smiles at CLARENCE.

SITTING BULL:
>   And you feel that way too. See? We are not so much
>   different.

CLARENCE:
>   Don't you think, maybe, you could think about goin'
>   back? Everybody hungry and everythin'. Is it worth
>   it?

SITTING BULL:
>   Across the line, on the reservations, they are starving
>   too. We hear these things and so must your people.

>   *CLARENCE nods.*

>   The white man is afraid to kill us outright, but he
>   knows if he kills the buffalo, we must soon follow.
>   ...I myself do not understand why you should wish
>   this on us.

CLARENCE:
>   I don't wish nothin' like that.

SITTING BULL:
>   And I think... if you give me nothing and you will
>   not let me go where I can get something for myself,
>   what is there? I would rather die fighting than die of
>   starvation.

CLARENCE: *uneasy*
>   You'd just all get killed that way.

SITTING BULL:
>   Yes. That is the warrior's way out... but I am not
>   only a warrior. I must think of *all* my people. I must
>   think of the ones here now and the ones that come
>   after... what is best for them.... I know we must
>   change.

CLARENCE:
>   Yeah. I guess that's it.

SITTING BULL:

allusion to Walsh as well

Sometimes one has something of value. Dogs come and spoil it for you, yet you do not wish to see it destroyed. . . . I am of the Hunkpapa Sioux of the prairie and the prairie will provide for me. When the buffalo are gone, my children will hunt mice. When my horse falls, I shall chase gopher. And when there is nothing else, we shall dig and eat roots. . . . And I pray to the Great Spirit that the White Mother gives the thought to her children that I give to mine.

We hear WALSH laughing harshly. The lights dim on SITTING BULL and CLARENCE and come up on WALSH, who is seated, looking at a letter. He rips the letter in half. McCUTCHEON is going through some papers. He concentrates on his business. He knows what's coming and he is preparing himself for it.

WALSH:

Why is nothing simple in this life? It all seems perfectly simple to me. Why do people make it complex? The simplest thing . . . complex.
. . . McCutcheon! Are you listening to me?

McCUTCHEON:

Aye, sir.

WALSH:

Well then, why is everything so goddamn complex?

McCUTCHEON:

I don't know, sir.

WALSH leaps up and begins to pace.

WALSH:

I write a report . . . a perfectly simple report . . . in which I state that our Indians as well as the Sioux are suffering severe deprivation because of the extinction of the buffalo. Is that simple or is that not?

McCUTCHEON:
> Perfectly simple, sir.

WALSH:
> Right! And if we do not make a sincere and whole-hearted effort to aid these Indians, we can expect trouble, necessitating a build-up in troops, horses and supplies, plus the possibility of loss of life as well as property.... And what is the government's reply to this?

McCUTCHEON:
> I don't know, sir.

WALSH: *exploding*
> The son-of-a-bitch's going to send me more men! And, to top it all off, I'll probably get a recommendation for my foresight!

> *CLARENCE enters with some papers. WALSH takes the papers.*

> Were you in court yesterday?

CLARENCE:
> No, sir.

WALSH:
> I sat in judgement yesterday. I sat in judgement of a Sioux. His wife and child were starving. He slaughtered a cow belonging to a settler and then....

> *He laughs. CLARENCE looks nervously, quickly, to McCUTCHEON, then back to WALSH.*

> Do you know what the damn fool did?

CLARENCE:
> No, sir, I....

WALSH:

He took his horse . . . his only horse . . . told the settler what had happened and offered the horse in payment. The settler refused and pressed charges. And yesterday, I sentenced that Sioux to six months imprisonment and fined him twenty dollars, for that is the law! But where's the justice in it?

LOUIS enters. WALSH turns on him and barks.

What is it?

There is a quick look between LOUIS and McCUTCHEON.

For God's sake, man, did you come in here to gape? Speak up!

LOUIS:

Sittin' Bull's outside.

WALSH stares at LOUIS for a moment, then he becomes very calm. He sits in a chair, picks up a pencil and begins to examine it.

WALSH:

And why is Sitting Bull's geographical location suppose to be of interest to me?

LOUIS:

He wants to see you.

WALSH:

I'm busy.

LOUIS stares hard at WALSH.

LOUIS:

I sent him on in!

He turns to go.

WALSH:
Louis!

LOUIS stops.

Just . . . give me a minute.

LOUIS exits. WALSH puts his pencil down, looks at McCUTCHEON and CLARENCE, then turns around and does up the top button of his tunic. His shoulders stiffen. SITTING BULL enters. WALSH has his back to him. LOUIS follows SITTING BULL in. SITTING BULL has a ragged blanket wrapped around him. He looks gaunt; not well, although his personal magnetism is still evident. He stops and looks at WALSH's back.

SITTING BULL:
White Sioux. . . .

WALSH: *without turning*
Yes.

SITTING BULL:
I wish to speak with you.

WALSH turns and looks at him.

WALSH:
I'm listening.

SITTING BULL:
Have you had news from the Great White Mother?

WALSH:
My news is always the same. . . . No reservations, no food, no clothing, no supplies.

SITTING BULL:
I wish you to send the Great White Mother a special message from Sitting Bull.

WALSH:
What is it?

SITTING BULL:
Tell her... once I was strong and brave. My people
had hearts of iron.... But now, my women are sick,
my children are freezing and I have thrown my war
paint to the wind. The suffering of my people has
made my heart weak and I have placed nothing in
the way of those who wish to return across the line.
Many have done so. We who remain desire a home.
For three years, we have been in the White Mother's
land. We have obeyed her laws and we have kept her
peace.... I beg the White Mother to... to...

WALSH:
Go on.

SITTING BULL:
... to have... pity... on us.

WALSH:
Right!... Well then... I'll see that this goes off....

SITTING BULL makes no move to leave.

Is there anything else?

SITTING BULL: *gazing at WALSH*
White Sioux...

WALSH:
Yes?

SITTING BULL: *speaking slowly and with effort*
... I find it necessary... to make a request...

WALSH stares at him.

... a request... for... provisions for my people.
We have nothing.

111

WALSH: *brusquely*
> Your provisions wait for you across the line. If you
> want provisions, go there for them.

SITTING BULL:
> We hear you have a quantity of flour and I have
> come to ask you for it.

WALSH:
> If you wish to do business, you do it at the trading
> post.

> *SITTING BULL takes off his ragged blanket. He holds*
> *out the blanket to WALSH. WALSH begins to breathe*
> *heavily as he struggles to retain control of himself.*

> I have appealed to the Great White Mother and the
> Great White Mother says no.

SITTING BULL:
> I ask for only a little.

WALSH: *exploding*
> And I can give you nothing! God knows, I've done
> my damndest and nothing's changed. Do you hear
> that? Nothing's changed! Cross the line if you're so
> hungry, but don't, for Christ's sake, come begging
> food from me!

SITTING BULL: *straightening up*
> You are speaking to the head of the Sioux nation!

WALSH:
> I don't give a goddamn who you are! Get the hell
> out!

> *SITTING BULL goes for the knife in his belt.*
> *WALSH grabs him by the arm, twists it up and throws*
> *him to the floor. As SITTING BULL goes to get up,*
> *WALSH puts his foot in the middle of his back and*
> *shoves him, sending him sprawling. He plants his foot*

in the middle of his back. CLARENCE and
McCUTCHEON enter.

CLARENCE: *screaming*
Nooooooooo!

> *McCUTCHEON grabs CLARENCE. Everyone freezes*
> *for a moment.*

WALSH: *in a strained voice*
McCutcheon, Underhill, go out and alert the boys in
case of trouble. Throw a couple of poles across the
road.

McCUTCHEON:
Yes, sir.

> *He starts off.*

Laddie!

> *CLARENCE looks at him. McCUTCHEON speaks*
> *more gently to him.*

Come on, laddie.

> *He takes CLARENCE off.*

The Major's given an order.

> *LOUIS steps forward and pushes WALSH aside. He*
> *still has his foot in the middle of SITTING BULL's*
> *back. LOUIS starts to help SITTING BULL up, but*
> *SITTING BULL gets up by himself. LOUIS gets him*
> *his blanket. SITTING BULL picks up his knife.*
> *He stands there staring at WALSH. There is a pause.*
> *SITTING BULL replaces his knife in its sheath.*
> *WALSH's hand slowly reaches out to SITTING BULL*
> *as SITTING BULL slowly turns, takes his blanket and*
> *exits. LOUIS stares at WALSH.*

LOUIS:
Is dat all for me, too?

*WALSH looks up at him for a moment, then slowly
nods his head. LOUIS exits. The sound of "Garryowen"
is heard faintly in the background. It builds as WALSH
straightens up and walks off. McCUTCHEON and
CLARENCE march on, carrying a trunk. They drop
it — bang — as the music ends. On the trunk is written:
Major James Walsh, NWMP, No. 7 Garden Lane,
Brockville, Ontario.*

CLARENCE:
I've never seen a trunk so roped up. What's he got
in it?

McCUTCHEON:
When the Major says securely fastened, he means
securely fastened.

CLARENCE:
I'd say that were excessive. You don't need that much
rope. It's a waste.

McCUTCHEON:
If you want to get on in the force, laddie, know your
place. The Major decrees the tying. I oversee the
tying . . . and you tie.

CLARENCE:
Yes, Sergeant.

McCUTCHEON:
Now get on over to the post and saddle up.

CLARENCE:
When's the Major leaving?

McCUTCHEON:
Later.

CLARENCE:
>I'd like to speak to him before he goes.

McCUTCHEON:
>Sorry, Constable.

CLARENCE:
>I've got to see him!

>*WALSH approaches the two of them. They do not see him.*

McCUTCHEON:
>Move your ass on over to that post!

CLARENCE:
>I can't go till I see him!

>*WALSH coughs.*

McCUTCHEON:
>Constable!

>*CLARENCE straightens to attention. WALSH glares at McCUTCHEON for not getting rid of CLARENCE, then he looks to the trunk.*

WALSH:
>Ah, good.

CLARENCE:
>Thank you, sir.

WALSH:
>Bit too much rope, perhaps.

CLARENCE: *with a brief look to McCUTCHEON*
>Yes, sir.

>*WALSH taps one of the lashings of rope with his riding crop.*

WALSH:
  This, I think, can go.

  CLARENCE gets down on his hands and knees.

CLARENCE:
  Yes, sir.

WALSH:
  You may go, Sergeant. . . .

  McCUTCHEON exits.

  A thing worth doing is worth doing well. . . . May
  take more time, but that's not the point, is it?

CLARENCE:
  No, sir.

WALSH:
  You wanted to speak to me?

CLARENCE:
  Yes, sir, I did. . . . Me and the men . . . a lot of us is
  upset, sir, about your leaving. . . .

WALSH:
  A simple leave of absence, Constable. I have a wife
  and children. It's been several years since I've seen
  them. Colonel MacLeod, upon my request, has
  kindly arranged several months off for me.

CLARENCE:
  It all seemed kinda sudden.

WALSH:
  I need the rest, Constable.

  He regrets his statement. He moves around the trunk.

The lettering's not quite right.... Had to have it
redone.... Been a long time since it's been in
transit.

CLARENCE:
There's something else.

WALSH:
Yes?

CLARENCE:
It's about Sitting Bull.

WALSH:
You see a lot of him.... The little boy, rather.

CLARENCE:
Yes, sir, I do. He's a very smart little boy and I have
a lot of hope for the Sioux when I talk to him, sir.

WALSH:
Do you?

CLARENCE:
Sitting Bull still considers you his friend.

WALSH:
I would have to deny that. I have my men and my
wife and children... but I have no friends. Friends
are a danger. You may not comprehend that
statement, Constable, but Sitting Bull would.

CLARENCE:
Maybe what I should have said was I still considered
you his friend. I know you've seen me out with food
and stuff, sir... and you haven't hauled me
up.... I'm not much good at sneaking.

WALSH:
That's true. I would never send you out on
reconnaissance.

He laughs.

CLARENCE:
No, sir.

WALSH:
What do you want to see me about, Constable?

CLARENCE:
You're goin' East to Brockville, sir. That's not too far
from Ottawa. I know you've been doin' all you can
from this end, but I just wondered if maybe you
couldn't go up to Ottawa and tell the Prime Minister
how things are. It'd make a difference. You'd make
him do something.

WALSH:
Oh yes.

CLARENCE:
Will you try and help Sittin' Bull?

WALSH:
I shall give your proposition every consideration.

McCUTCHEON:
Sorry to interrupt, sir, but. . . .

WALSH:
Quite right. I must get on, Constable.

CLARENCE:
Can I tell Sittin' Bull that?

WALSH:
Our chat has been most informative, Constable.
No doubt I'll see you on my return.

CLARENCE exits.

Your timing is impeccable, McCutcheon.

McCUTCHEON:
> I know, sir.

WALSH:
> The trunk looks solid, don't you think?

McCUTCHEON:
> Aye, sir.

> *WALSH looks after CLARENCE.*

WALSH:
> That young man should never make the force his life.

> *He looks at McCUTCHEON and exits. The lights
> dim. SITTING BULL enters. He rolls up his buffalo
> robe and looks at PRETTY PLUME and
> CROWFOOT. The lights come up on HARRY, who
> has a bottle and who is singing.*

HARRY:
> Oh, life in a prairie shack, when the rain begins to
> pour.
> Drip, drip, it comes through the roof and I want to
> go home to my Ma — Maw.
> Maw, Maw, I want to go home to my Maw.
> This bloomin' country's a fraud and I want to go
> home to my Maw.

> *CLARENCE enters from one direction, carrying a
> cup; LOUIS and McCUTCHEON enter from the
> other direction.*

LOUIS:
> Alors, je lui dirais, mange la merde!

McCUTCHEON:
> It's the pay, mostly . . . very poor pay, ye could
> say. . . .

LOUIS:
Mange la merde!

McCUTCHEON:
And nobody gives a damn!

CLARENCE:
Shut up! This bloody bastard's talkin' French and
you're talkin' at the same goddamn time. You make
me dizzy!

They fall silent—and drink. There is a pause, then
CLARENCE speaks quietly.

Where's the Major?

LOUIS:
Eh?

McCUTCHEON:
Never mind him, Louis.

CLARENCE: *louder*
Where the hell's the goddamn Major?

McCUTCHEON:
He's not here.

CLARENCE:
I know he's not here. What kind of a fool do you take
me for? I know he's not here.

McCUTCHEON:
Give me another, Louis.

CLARENCE:
What kind of a leave of absence is eighteen months?
That's what I want to know.

LOUIS pours McCUTCHEON another drink. He
looks at CLARENCE.

McCUTCHEON:
>He's had enough.

He leans toward CLARENCE.

>You've had enough, Clarence!

HARRY: *singing*
>This bloomin' country's a fraud and I want to go
>home to my Maw.

McCUTCHEON:
>Come on, y'old buzzard. Sit down and shut up!

HARRY: *coming over*
>I want to go home to my Maw. . . . You boys been
>celebratin'?

CLARENCE:
>What?

McCUTCHEON:
>When did ye get in?

HARRY: *filling CLARENCE's cup*
>Done and over with. . . . Signed, sealed and delivered.
>I seen the last of Sittin' Bull.

CLARENCE:
>How'd it go?

HARRY:
>Me and five or six of the boys from C Troop, we
>escorted him down to the border with nary an
>incident. . . . The boys signed him over and then they
>came back up.

CLARENCE:
>Where was you?

HARRY:
Sittin' Bull, he asked me to go on down to Fort Robson with him. That's where they was gonna be picked up and taken over to the reservation.

CLARENCE:
Yeah?

HARRY:
So I did!

CLARENCE:
Everythin' go all right?

HARRY:
You know that old horse he was ridin'? Bluecoats took that and everythin' else. . . . Said they wouldn't be needing guns or horses where they was goin'.

CLARENCE:
I never seen a Sioux without some kind of horse standin' by.

He is insinuating that HARRY is a liar.

HARRY:
Yeah. . . well, they sure looked a sight. Real ragtag bunch, I'm tellin' you.

There is a pause as they drink.

CLARENCE:
How was they takin' them to the reservation with no horses?

HARRY:
Walkin' them . . . 'cept Sittin' Bull.

CLARENCE:
What about Sittin' Bull?

HARRY:

> They put him on some boat. Gonna take him down to Fort Randall.

CLARENCE:

> Fort Randall.

LOUIS:

> Dat's da military prison.

CLARENCE:

> Why's he goin' there?

HARRY:

> Why'd you think?

CLARENCE:

> The agreement was nobody'd be punished.   ⌐

> *There is a pause.*

> Ain't that right?

HARRY:

> I don't know nothin' 'bout what's right. . . . All's I know is that Sittin' Bull's in Fort Randall for killin' Custer.

CLARENCE:

> What . . . what'd he do when they told him?

HARRY:

> He said somethin' 'bout not goin' . . . not havin' to. . . . One of them bluecoats just give him a good clip on the side of the head with his rifle butt and they carried him aboard. . . . Weren't nothin' to it. Yessiree, I seen a historical sight. . . . I seen the end of the Sioux nation.

CLARENCE:

> That's not true!

HARRY:

>Was you there? . . . That boat moved off down the river and all them Injuns lined up along the bank makin' this terrible moanin' sound. I'm telling you, it was somethin' to see.

>>*There is a pause.*

>What's the matter with you bastards? Me, Harry, is gonna propose a toast!

>>*He holds up the bottle. LOUIS and McCUTCHEON hold up their glasses.*

>Here's to the Sioux! They won the battle, but they lost the war!

>>*CLARENCE throws his drink in HARRY's face. HARRY stands up and throws one punch at CLARENCE which knocks him cold. McCUTCHEON and LOUIS carry CLARENCE off. HARRY looks at the audience and proposes a toast.*

>Bottoms up!

>>*He drinks.*

>Sir John A.'s policy for dealin' with the Sioux was an all round winner . . . beats Custer all to hell! Not half so messy as ridin' into tube-like hollows at ungodly hours of the mornin' . . . and no need for a marchin' band. . . . Quiet, simple and effective. . . . Do not delay in returning to the United States, for that course is the only alternative to death by starvation. . . . So Sittin' Bull left the Canadian West . . .

>>*WALSH enters and stands behind his desk.*

>. . . and Major Walsh returned to it. Yessireee, beats Custer all to hell!

124

McCUTCHEON formally carries on a large board with a map on it; toy soldiers, a train engine, trees. HARRY looks at the board as McCUTCHEON puts it on WALSH's desk. HARRY laughs.

Je-sus!

He exits, shaking his head.

WALSH:

The railway track is here. . . . There is a slight curve here around a grove of trees. . . . Do you see that, McCutcheon?

McCUTCHEON:

Aye, sir.

WALSH:

I think possibly twenty men could be concealed amongst those trees . . . twenty men. . . . Do we have twenty men we can rely on? Top notch fellows?

RCMP reduced to enforcement spectacle

McCUTCHEON:

Aye, sir.

WALSH:

Good. In an operation like this, there is no room for error. . . . Image of the force and all that. . . . So . . . the men are concealed here.

He taps the map.

At 2:10 precisely, the train should round this curve. . . . You follow me?

McCUTCHEON:

Aye, sir.

WALSH:

All right. . . . Now, as the train reaches this point, Harry pulls out with a full load across the tracks. . . .

McCUTCHEON:
Isn't that a bit dangerous, sir?

WALSH looks at him sharply.

I mean, sir . . . will the train have ample time to stop, sir?

WALSH:
All that is calculated.

Speaking coldly.

Would you care to check my figures?

McCUTCHEON:
No, sir . . . just wondering.

WALSH: *staring at him*
Good.

He turns his attention back to the map.

Now, as the train pulls up, the men, myself at the head. . . . There'll be a dress parade before . . . I told you that, didn't I?

McCUTCHEON:
Aye, sir.

WALSH:
Right! . . . I will ride out from the woods, my men behind me, and all of us in full dress. . . . Tell the men to practice war whoops. I want good full-blooded Indian yells, you hear?

McCUTCHEON:
Aye, sir.

WALSH:
> So, out we come... yelling bloody murder.... I'll
> swing aboard the train and ride it into Calgary. Well,
> what do you think? Is that a stirring sight or not?

McCUTCHEON:
> Very stirring, sir.

WALSH:
> When you open a railroad, you do it in style, I say!
> Bloody train will be full of Easterners and we'll scare
> the pants off every one of them! I want a good show!

> *CLARENCE enters, followed by LOUIS.*

CLARENCE:
> Major.

WALSH: *stopping him*
> Underhill! You have interruped an important
> conference!

CLARENCE:
> Beggin' your pardon, sir.... Request permission to
> speak, sir.

WALSH: *long suffering*
> What is it?

CLARENCE:
> A rider's come in from Standin' Rock.... Been in the
> saddle all night.

WALSH:
> And?

LOUIS:
> He's dead.... Da white man have da Indian Police
> kill 'im.... Sittin' Bull is dead!... Da rider say he see
> his face bleed empty and death come starin' in its
> place.

CLARENCE:
> They shot him twice and put the boots to him . . . and
> Little Crow says the soldiers dropped him in a pit of
> lime, so's his people couldn't bury him proper.

> *WALSH stands there frozen, staring at CLARENCE.*

> And Crowfoot? . . . Do you remember Crowfoot, sir?
> He used to come up to the fort, sir, and us men, we
> used to play with him 'cause he was just a kid . . . and
> ain't none of us got kids here . . . and he was a real
> good boy . . . and I liked him, sir. . . . And they drug
> him out from under the bed where he was hidin' and
> they threw him down and they shot him and he's
> dead too!

> *His anger is spent.*

> I come in to tell you, sir . . . 'cause . . . 'cause . . .
> I didn't know what else to do.

> *WALSH stands so still he seems to be a statue.*
> *There is a long pause. At last, he speaks.*

WALSH:
> Dis-missed. . . .

> *McCUTCHEON, LOUIS and CLARENCE make no*
> *move to leave.*

DIS-MISSED!

> *They exit. WALSH watches them leave. He moves to his*
> *desk and looks at it. He undoes his leather holster and*
> *takes out his gun. As he does this, we hear the sound of*
> *the Nez Percés from the end of Act One. That sound*
> *continues as he lays the gun on the desk and slowly,*
> *carefully, takes off his tunic, putting it on the desk as*
> *well. We hear SITTING BULL's voice as WALSH*
> *slowly lifts both hands over his head. SITTING BULL*

speaks softly, reminiscent of his speech to CROWFOOT early in Act Two.

SITTING BULL:

In the beginning... was given... to everyone a cup.... A cup of clay. And from this cup, we drink our life. We all dip in the water... but the cups are different.... My cup is broken. It has passed away.

WALSH slams his hands down on his desk.

Blackout.

TALONBOOKS—PLAYS IN PRINT 1983

The Primary English Class — Israel Horovitz
Jitters — David French
Aléola — Gaëtan Charlebois
After Abraham — Ron Chudley
Sainte-Marie Among the Hurons — James W. Nichol
The Lionel Touch — George Hulme
Balconville — David Fennario
Maggie & Pierre — Linda Griffiths with Paul Thompson
Waiting for the Parade — John Murrell
The Twilight Dinner & Other Plays — Lennox Brown
Sainte-Carmen of the Main — Michel Tremblay
Damnée Manon, Sacrée Sandra — Michel Tremblay
The Impromptu of Outremont — Michel Tremblay
Billy Bishop Goes to War — John Gray with Eric Peterson
Cold Comfort — Jim Garrard
The Fairies Are Thirsty — Denise Boucher

TALONBOOKS — THEATRE FOR THE YOUNG

Raft Baby — Dennis Foon
The Windigo — Dennis Foon
Heracles — Dennis Foon
A Chain of Words — Irene N. Watts
Apple Butter — James Reaney
Geography Match — James Reaney
Names and Nicknames — James Reaney
Ignoramus — James Reaney
A Teacher's Guide to Theatre for Young People — Jane Howard Baker
A Mirror of Our Dreams — Joyce Doolittle and Zina Barnich